Advance Praise

A Woman's Job draws our attention through its rich ethnographic work to the narratives, life-stories of young women who move between various jobs to create a particular identity and representation of themselves as not quite middle class or working class, but somewhere in between. This *in-between-ness*, which the author calls 'mid-identification', opens up fresh ways to look at actions, consciousness and motivations of new classes of working women. It will make a great addition to scholarship on work, gender and labour.

Madhumita Dutta
Author of *Mobile Girls Koottam: Working Women Speak*

Ideas and definitions around the meaning of 'work' are much enriched by this engaging and beautifully written study of young women in contemporary Delhi. The connections between public and private worlds and old and new cultures are brought to life by women attempting to negotiate their social spaces. In the best possible way, this study allows its subjects to speak and enables readers to recognise the tangled patterns around the concept of work.

Mary Evans
Author of *Making Respectable Women: Changing Moralities,*
Changing Times

By focusing on the lower-middle-class status of young women workers, positioned at the intersection of traditional values and modern aspirations, the book highlights a crucial yet often overlooked segment of society whose experiences and struggles are pivotal to understanding the broader dynamics of social change in urban contexts. *A Woman's Job* is an essential read for anyone seeking to understand young women's everyday negotiations of the evolving demands of the labour market and enduring gender norms in Indian society.

Naila Kabeer
Author of *Renegotiating Patriarchy: Gender,*
Agency and the Bangladesh Paradox

Written as a beautiful play led by intriguing lead characters, *A Woman's Job* shows the power of 'middle-ness' as field and method for research enquiry into the gendered social world of the everyday. The result is a powerful ethnography into middle-class-ness as aspiration, familial sacrifice and learnt practice, performed

by the young women of 'Shining India'. Asiya Islam offers us truly a great read, exploring the extraordinary structural transformation of contemporary India through the ordinary rhythms of daily life-making.

Alessandra Mezzadri
Author of *The Sweatshop Regime: Labouring Bodies, Exploitation, and Garments Made in India*

A compelling insight into how the complex relations of class, caste, gender and sexuality shape the material desires and cultural challenges of a lively group of young women as they craftily negotiate traditional limits and modernity to generate space for a more interesting life. The reader is drawn into the environment, wanting to know what they will do next. An ethnographic and theoretical challenge.

Beverley Skeggs
Author of *Formations of Class and Gender: Becoming Respectable*

A Woman's Job

Against the backdrop of rapid socio-economic change in post-1990 India, scholars and policymakers have expressed surprise at the low rate of women's participation in the workforce, particularly in urban areas. *A Woman's Job* presents a unique urban ethnography of young lower-middle-class women's lives in Delhi as they weave in and out of service employment, education and domestic contracts. Urban, educated and skilled, these young women seek employment in cafés, malls, call centres and offices in the globalising landscape of Delhi. Their participation in work enables access to 'things', such as jeans, smartphones, the English language and the metro, which symbolise global modernity. However, caught in a web of gender, class and caste inequalities, their identification as 'working' women also generates social anxieties. The book shows how women adopt 'middle-ness' as a strategy of life-making at the multiple sites of work, home and leisure.

Asiya Islam is Assistant Professor of Gender, Development and Globalisation at the London School of Economics and Political Science. Her research on gender, work and digital technologies has been funded by the Gates Cambridge Scholarship, the British Academy and the Economic and Social Research Council (ESRC)-funded Digital Futures at Work Research Centre (Digit). She has published widely, including in the journals *Gender and Society*, *Gender, Work and Organization* and *Sociology*.

SOUTH ASIA IN THE SOCIAL SCIENCES

South Asia has become a laboratory for devising new institutions and practices of modern social life. Forms of capitalist enterprise, providing welfare and social services, the public role of religion, the management of ethnic conflict, popular culture and mass democracy in the countries of the region have shown a marked divergence from known patterns in other parts of the world. South Asia is now being studied for its relevance to the general theoretical understanding of modernity itself.

South Asia in the Social Sciences features books that offer innovative research on contemporary South Asia. It focuses on the place of the region in the various global disciplines of the social sciences and highlights research that uses unconventional sources of information and novel research methods. While recognising that most current research is focused on the larger countries, the series attempts to showcase research on the smaller countries of the region.

General Editor
Partha Chatterjee
Columbia University

Editorial Board
Stuart Corbridge
Durham University

Satish Deshpande
University of Delhi (retired)

Christophe Jaffrelot
Centre d'etudes et de recherches internationales, Paris

Nivedita Menon
Jawaharlal Nehru University

Books in the series:

Government as Practice: Democratic Left in a Transforming India
Dwaipayan Bhattacharyya

Courting the People: Public Interest Litigation in Post-Emergency India
Anuj Bhuwania

A Woman's Job

Making Middle Lives in New India

Asiya Islam

CAMBRIDGE
UNIVERSITY PRESS

Shaftesbury Road, Cambridge CB2 8EA, United Kingdom

One Liberty Plaza, 20th Floor, New York, NY 10006, USA

477 Williamstown Road, Port Melbourne, VIC 3207, Australia

314–321, 3rd Floor, Plot 3, Splendor Forum, Jasola District Centre, New Delhi – 110025, India

103 Penang Road, #05–06/07, Visioncrest Commercial, Singapore 238467

Cambridge University Press is part of Cambridge University Press & Assessment, a department of the University of Cambridge.

We share the University's mission to contribute to society through the pursuit of education, learning and research at the highest international levels of excellence.

www.cambridge.org
Information on this title: www.cambridge.org/9781009536653

First published 2024

Printed in India by Repro India Ltd.

A catalogue record for this publication is available from the British Library

ISBN 978-1-009-53665-3 Paperback

For my grandfather, Khurshidul Islam, who (I am pretty sure)
was the first person to tell me that one day I will be a writer

Contents

Figures

Acknowledgements

I love reading, writing, and editing, especially when I can do it free of other commitments of academic life. For that, I have to credit my junior research fellowship at Newnham College, University of Cambridge, which allowed me not only the time to immerse myself into book writing, but also the luxury of creative and exploratory thinking, an increasingly rare affordance in university life. This time was enriched by the brilliant company of Opening Lines, a writers' group for those writing their first book. Supported by CRASSH (Centre for Research in the Arts, Social Sciences and Humanities) at the University of Cambridge, particularly Nicki Dawidowski, and mentored by Jenny Chamarette, the group of a dozen scholars writing their first books provided generous peer review and what we all came to understand as 'friendly accountability'. I would be lucky to find such an academic community again.

The book has travelled miles from my doctoral thesis, but the PhD is what enabled it in the first place. The Gates Cambridge Scholarship, much like the fellowship at Newnham College, gave me the gift of time and resources for this research. Thank you to Professor Manali Desai for her patient guidance over the years and for articulating the significance of my research at times when I found it difficult to do so. I am also hugely grateful to Professor Sarah Franklin and Professor Mary Evans for their faith in my work that they have kindly shown in various ways, including by reviewing my drafts, offering advice and writing many references! I had the privilege of having my thesis examined by two scholars whose work inspired my research: Professor Beverley Skeggs and Professor Samita Sen. In the writing of this book, I have continued to turn to Skeggs' *Formations of Class and Gender: Becoming Respectable* (1997) and Sen's *Women and Labour in Late Colonial India: The Bengal Jute Industry* (1999) as examples of brilliant feminist scholarship that I aspire to. And then there are friends who shape my understanding of gender (and are always happy to talk to me about it!) – thank you, Gavin Stevenson, Jana Bacevic, Shannon Philip, Hatice Yildiz.

My family has thankfully not annoyed me by continually asking when the book will be out – only periodically (and in a supportive way). All my love to Arvind for patiently telling me to not miss the wood for the trees. And to my parents for their absolute (slightly scary) confidence in me; Abba kept me company in Goa as I completed the first draft of the book, and Amma asked if she could read it, which encouraged me to actually get it done. My sisters – Saadia and Sophiya – were excellent travel companions on our trip to Hanoi, which helped me to recharge and return to finalising the manuscript. And if that was not enough, I now also have Sheeba John and J. John telling me how proud they are of me – thank you.

Anwesha Rana and Qudsiya Ahmed have been wonderful editors, from showing an interest in the book to making the publication process smooth, being gentle and yet persuasive about deadlines. I am also grateful for the three reviewers who took the time to read the full manuscript and offer comments; the final version of the manuscript was improved by their feedback. Parts of my papers published in the journals *Sociology*, *Gender and Society* and *Ethnography* and a chapter published by Bristol University Press appear in the book – thank you to the editors of these publications for sending out my work for review.

Finally, but most importantly, I thank the women in Delhi who agreed to be part of this research, who shared their life stories with me – I hope I have done justice to their accounts in the book. A special thanks to my wonderful 'Delhi friends' who I do not get to see as much as I would like to: Pooja, Sunita and Chinu.

Note on anonymisation and translation

Throughout the book, I have changed names of people to ensure anonymisation. Additionally, I have given pseudonyms to two skill training centres. The pseudonyms I chose are in keeping with the original names, reflecting the genders and castes of people and the character of skill training centres. I have, however, not assigned any pseudonyms to workplaces, instead choosing to not use any names for specific workplaces at all. While it would have been near impossible to trace the workers even if the workplaces were identified, I decided not to do so for two interrelated reasons: (*a*) I contacted workers individually and through their friend networks, not through their workplaces; as such, I did not, at any point, seek permission from owners or managers for this research, instead conducting it largely outside of workplaces; (*b*) the workers changed work fairly often, rendering the specific characteristics of these workplaces, whilst not irrelevant, unimportant.

All the conversations and interviews were conducted primarily in Hindi, with a smattering of English words, phrases and sometimes sentences. I translated and transcribed the recorded conversations and interviews and wrote field notes in English. I have retained the original uses of English in the transcription and notes, marking them through italicisation throughout and emphasising where they were of particular significance. Notably, all the chapter titles in the book are English words that were in circulation as terms to signify or describe emerging gendered youth subjectivities.

Cast of characters
(in order of appearance)

Main cast

Sheela
Sheela was a barista at a café, which was her first job. She studied up to class 12, or pre-university level. She wanted to study further but did not have enough money to enrol into an undergraduate distance learning programme as many of her peers had done. She lived with her parents and three younger siblings. Her mother worked as a domestic worker in multiple households, while her father was unemployed.

Prachi
Prachi worked as barista at the same café as Sheela and quit the job soon after I met her. She was unemployed for a period of time, worked as my research assistant for a few months and later found work in an office. She was enrolled in a distance learning Bachelor of Arts (BA) programme (offered by Delhi University). She lived with her parents and four siblings. Her mother worked as a masseuse, but this was not a regular source of income; her father was long-term unemployed.

Jahanvi
Jahanvi had experience of working at cafés: her first job was at a doughnut place in Select Citywalk, New Delhi, and she was working at a specialty tea café (in the same mall) when I met her. She had two younger sisters; she lived with them and her parents, who worked as *press wallah*s, ironing clothes, which is what her grandparents had also done. She mentioned her best friend – Neeraj – frequently,

who was her 'partner in crime'. Neeraj lent her money when needed, helped convince her father to let her work and went on trips with her. As others, Jahanvi was also pursuing a BA degree through distance learning.

Chandni

Chandni was unemployed when I first met her. She had a wide-ranging work experience: her first job, straight out of school, was in a call centre, followed by a job in an office, and a short stint at the same café as Sheela and Prachi, where the three became friends. After quitting from the café, she was unemployed for a short while. She then started doing ad hoc 'events' and 'promotions' work for various car and mobile companies; she also participated in market research groups as a source of income. She was pursuing a BA degree through distance learning. Her mother took up work as a nanny for a certain period of time; her father was unemployed.

Priya

Priya was Prachi's younger sister. She was unemployed when I first met her; she then found a job as a sales assistant at a grocery store in Select Citywalk. She had completed a personality development course at a neighbourhood skill training centre. She lived with her parents and four siblings.

Ranjini

Ranjini worked at a fast-food outlet at Select Citywalk and had two years' work experience when I met her. She had secured this job through the skill training centre where she had done a course on employability skills. She lived with her parents and brother. Her father worked as a driver, while her mother worked as a sales assistant in a clothes shop.

Deepti

Deepti was Prachi's friend from school. She worked as a barista at multinational café. She was pursuing a BA degree through distance learning. She had also done a computer course and undergone teachers' training. She lived with her parents and brother. Her father worked as a delivery person, delivering goods from a factory to shops; her mother was a 'housewife' but had previously worked in a factory too as a 'checker'.

Anamika

Anamika was Prachi's elder sister. She had only studied up to class 5 due to financial problems faced by the family following her father's unemployment.

Unable to enter the new service economy – as her sisters, Prachi and Priya, had done – she worked part-time as a helper at a boutique run at home by someone the family had known and worked with for a long time.

Pranjali

Pranjali worked as financial assistant at a small architecture firm. She was studying Bachelor of Commerce (BCom) (also distance learning). She lived with her parents and two siblings. Her father worked as a *mistri*, or mason (daily wage labour), and her mother was a 'housewife'.

Chitra

Chitra was Chandni's close friend. She had worked at the call centre with Chandni; they quit together, and then did ad hoc 'events' and 'promotions' work together again. Frustrated by lack of stability, she eventually quit work altogether. Her father was disabled and unemployed; her mother was a housewife, although she had previously worked in an undergarment shop in a local market. Her brother worked as a driver but did not regularly contribute an income to the household.

Aarti

Aarti worked in the stationery room of a telecoms company. She had previously worked in small offices and had experience of graphic design. She was enrolled in a BA programme via distance learning through which she became friends with Prachi. She lived with her parents and three siblings. Her father worked in a shop that sold gas cylinders; her mother was a housewife; her elder sister worked as a schoolteacher.

Meeta

Meeta worked at a café, which was her first job. She lived with her parents and four siblings. Her father worked as a supervisor in a small hotel; her mother was a housewife; her sisters had finished studying but did not work; her brothers were still studying.

Sarita

Sarita was Jahanvi's colleague at the doughnut café in Select Citywalk. She had moved on to another café in the mall when I met her. She was pursuing a Master of Arts (MA) degree through distance learning. She had previously enrolled into, but not completed, a computer course at a neighbourhood skill training centre. She lived with her parents and three siblings. Her father worked as a rickshaw puller, while her mother was a domestic worker. Her elder brother and sister were unemployed, and her younger brother was still studying.

Neha

Neha worked as a sales assistant at a lifestyle shop in Select Citywalk. She was enrolled in a BA programme (distance learning). She had previously done a sewing course at the local women's training centre (Mahila Mandal). She was engaged to be married. She lived with her parents and three siblings. Her father worked as a supervisor in a newspaper delivery agency.

Supporting cast

Soniya

Soniya was Jahanvi's neighbour. She used to work at a fast-food outlet but had quit to pursue fashion designing. She also provided private tuitions at home to earn a stable income.

Mahesh

Mahesh was the manager of a skill training centre.

Aradhna

Aradhna worked as a teacher and mobiliser for a non-governmental organisation (NGO).

Rama

Rama worked as a domestic worker. A single mother, she lived with her eight-year-old son.

Sarla

Sarla was unemployed. She had previously undertaken training in beauty parlour work and sewing, but she never secured employment.

1

A woman's job

The Select Citywalk mall in South Delhi occupies 1.3 million square feet of prime land. A Quora search reveals that that is equivalent to almost 21 football fields, 40 White Houses and 10 Walmart stores. Its looming glass building houses international brands – Zara, H&M, UNIQLO, Sephora, Dior, MAC, Burger King, KFC – providing an 'upscale' shopping experience. Its air-conditioned and gleaming interiors with high ceilings and spotless (somewhat slippery) floors open on to an expansive landscaped plaza, featuring tropical palms, fountains and a giant-sized statue of the Buddha. On a regular evening, it is not uncommon to see people, especially couples, sitting on the steps in the landscaped plaza of the mall, making it a convenient dating spot. The epithets 'out of this world' and 'larger than life' seem fitting for the mall that towers above and pushes out its surroundings. The year Select Citywalk opened – 2007 – falls in the early period of the emergence of malls in India, following the opening of the economy to global trade in the 1990s. In the first decade of the 21st century, malls were still a novelty, but by the end of the second decade, they became a much more common feature, alongside cafés, call centres and high-rise offices, transforming the urban Indian landscape. These spaces signify the advent of a global culture that has influenced the social fabric of urban India and, perhaps most remarkably, altered the desires, attitudes and aspirations of the youth, who comprise 'liberalization's children' (Lukose 2009).

Popular discourse suggests that the socio-economic changes of the last three decades have offered urban young Indians the opportunity to join the ranks of an expanding 'new middle class'. While there are contestations over the size of the new middle class, with critics suggesting that the statistical significance of the new middle class in India may be overestimated (Aslany 2019; Banerjee and Duflo 2008), sociologists and anthropologists have delved into what characterises this new middle class and indeed whether there is anything 'new' about it. Leela Fernandes (2000: 90) argues that rather than expanding, it is the cultural basis of the middle class that has shifted so that the new middle class is, in the context of liberalisation, invented as 'the social group which is able to negotiate India's new relationship with the global economy in both cultural and economic terms'. Similarly, Ritty Lukose (2009: 6) suggests that the new middle class is the 'new globalised generation' that 'admires capitalism and wants to get rich … is technology savvy, consumes guiltlessly … favors jobs in the private corporate sector, and has higher literacy rates'. The 'newness' of the post-1990 new middle class is then, in part, closely linked to the expansion of the service economy and the employment opportunities it supposedly offers to the Indian youth. However, in contrast to the popular imagination of young Indians working in well-paid jobs in private multinational companies, the reality of emerging middle-class lives, scholars have pointed out, is characterised by precarity and insecurity, replicating conditions in the informal economy (Fernandes 2006; Ganguly-Scrase and Scrase 2009; Gooptu 2013).

Against the glitzy picture of malls, cafés and high-rises, there is a growing corpus of qualitative research on the lived realities of middle-class youth. Much of this scholarship focuses on the lives of young men, including emerging ideals of masculinity (Baas 2020; Philip 2022), their participation in 'globally familiar' cultures (Dattatreyan 2020), as well as frustration at the lack of life choices, suffering long-term unemployment and engaging in 'timepass' (Jeffrey 2010). Although there are emerging accounts of young women's practices of consumption, leisure and risk, particularly at the site of educational institutions (Krishnan 2022; Lukose 2009), enquiries into the opportunities afforded to women in the new service economy of India have been largely limited to studies of the information technology (IT) industry (Belliappa 2013; Patel 2010; Radhakrishnan 2011; Upadhya 2011; Vijayakumar 2013). As such, we know little about the lives, and indeed livelihoods, of the young women who are heavily present in discourses of globalisation and development – as (potential or already) victims of sexual violence, their bodies in public spaces rendered as antithesis to India's claims to modernity (John 2019; Raychowdhry 2013); as targets for development initiatives, such as microfinance (Radhakrishnan 2021) and family planning;

and as a latent workforce, with concern over the low and declining female labour force participation rate in India (Abraham 2013; Neetha 2014; Sudarshan and Bhattacharya 2009).

This book ethnographically attends to the everyday lives of those who could conveniently be categorised as 'modern Indian women' or 'new Indian women' (Dhawan 2010; Lau 2010; Oza 2006) – urban and educated young women seeking work in the expanding service economy in Delhi, working across cafés, call centres, shopping malls and offices. In contrast to the glamour of their workplaces, these women's residences are modest. Living in small one- or two-bedroom apartments with their families in the narrow lanes of Dakshinpuri, a neighbourhood in South Delhi, these women participate in 'crossing borders of class and neighbourhood from the lower class (and in all likelihood backward castes) world that forms their residences to the space of erotic bodies and hyper real images' (Johri and Menon 2014: 3; also see Sadana 2010). The book asks: What are the forces shaping these women's lives? Are they the same as those shaping young men's lives – that is, lack of economic opportunities, sexual violence as an assertion of masculinity, changing ideals of bodies? If so, how do they differentially impact and mould women coming of age? Or are they different forces – perhaps persevering ideas of domesticity, public–private divisions and competing pressures of traditions and modernity? Engaging with their narratives, the book is distinct in situating women at the centre of class formations, highlighting the ways in which women, rather than being passive recipients or maintainers of class, are at the forefront of mediating a new class politics. Rather than what Pierre Bourdieu (2010 [1984]) calls being 'taken in by the game', young women offer critique of the story of upward mobility, opportunities and aspirations in post-1990s urban India even as they participate in the game. Building on such women's narratives, the book moves beyond the category of new middle class, introducing the conceptual vocabulary of 'middle lives' and 'mid-identification' to understand both changes in and reproduction of entanglements of youth, gender, class and caste in the mise en scène of globalisation, development and modernity in India.

The working lives of women

In recent years, the low and declining female labour force participation rate in India[1] has attracted attention and concern, including from international development agencies, such as the International Labour Organization (Kapsos, Silberman and Bourmpoula 2014) and UN Women (Raveendran 2016). Even with the caveat that women's work may be underestimated (Sudarshan and Bhattacharya 2009), the female labour force participation rate in urban India is strikingly low; the Periodic Labour Force Survey's annual report of 2022–23 records this at 20.2 per cent (Ministry of Statistics and Programme Implementation 2023). While this is often posed as counterintuitive to globalisation and economic growth, Indrani Mazumdar (2007) rightly argues that to a certain extent these figures reflect men's migration for urban work opportunities and women's dispossession from agriculture *as a result of* globalisation and liberalisation. Of the small proportion of women in urban India who are in the workforce, most are concentrated in the service sector (Ministry of Statistics and Programme Implementation 2019).[2] This book gains relevance in this context and offers an ethnographic account where most research has relied on surveys. However, in this engagement, the book also sits with what I understand and articulate as feminist discomforts.

The first discomfort is the distinction between working and non-working women established in conducting a study with women in employment. This is, of course, grounded in feminist scholarship that criticises the enforced separation of paid or 'productive' work and unpaid or 'reproductive' work, arguing that 'the unwaged condition of housework has been the most powerful weapon in reinforcing the common assumption that housework is not work, thus preventing women from struggling against it' (Federici 2012 [1975]: 77). But it is also further grounded in scholarship on precarious work and precarity in the Global South that shows that the boundaries between work and non-work are blurry. Ben Scully (2016) illustrates, in the context of South Africa, that compelled by precarity, people aggregate multiple strategies to sustain livelihoods; these include both income-generating and non-income-generating activities. Similarly, in the edited volume *Beyond the Wage: Ordinary Work in Diverse Economies*, William Monteith, Dora-Olivia Vicol and Philippa Williams (2021: 11) put forth an expanded conceptualisation of work as 'ordinary' to offer 'an engagement with the ways in which it is experienced and understood in everyday life; its entanglement with other activities, relations and projects'. This finds resonance with the concept of 'diverse economies' in economic geography, which proposes that the economy extends beyond the visible to hidden, marginalised and alternative activities (Gibson-Graham 2008). In drawing a line between 'work' and 'non-work' on the basis of income generation, we thus risk neglecting a comprehensive understanding of people's everyday activities that sustain life. I find it useful to take up some of the relatively new languages of diverse economies, ordinary work and livelihood strategies together with feminist conceptualisations of social reproduction (T. Bhattacharya 2017; G. Bhattacharya 2018; Federici 2009; Mezzadri 2019) to frame this investigation as one into women's *working lives*, a framing that encompasses employment, education, domestic contracts as well as leisure as *life-making* activities. The title of the book – *A Woman's Job* – is a statement as much as a question about what makes something a woman's job, or, indeed, what constitutes a woman's job.

The second discomfort is with the association of women's employment with women's empowerment, predominant in development approaches that view women as latent capital for economic growth. Calls to mobilise employment for women are premised on the understanding that paid work is empowering and therefore a 'good thing' for women and for growing economies. While this understanding is not entirely unsubstantiated, it is nevertheless problematic. As Black feminists have pointed out, historically Black women laboured both inside and outside their homes, reproducing their own and White families, with very little to claim in terms of 'empowerment' (hooks 1984). Similarly, South Asian feminists have highlighted how forces of globalisation have turned women into subjects or objects of poverty alleviation and development through micro-credit schemes, garment factories, home-based work and conditional cash transfers at the cost of exploitation (John and Gopal 2021; Mohanty 1997).

Clearly, then, the question of women's employment has to be examined in confluence with social relations that organise labour, including class and caste, in the Indian context. Historically, a family's prosperity was indicated by women's confinement to domesticity. The association of respectability with women's relegation to the home produced through the colonial binary between the public and the private spheres implied that upwardly mobile families consolidated their status through women's withdrawal from employment (Banerjee 1990; Papanek 1979). Although this is still largely taken to be the case, there are indications that rather than women's confinement to the private sphere, women's presence in public spaces is becoming desirable, constitutive of upwardly mobile status and representative of modernity (Ganguly-Scrase 2003; also see Evans 2020 for a similar discussion in a different context). The book engages with this trend by focusing on 'lower-middle-class' women, those traversing the precarious line between the working poor and the secure middle class, whose participation in the workforce is at the crossroads of necessity and aspiration. It highlights the complexities of lower-middle-class women's decision-making around employment, in conjunction with education and skills training, leisure and domestic contracts. In doing so, the book particularly draws attention to women's narratives about inequalities and exploitation, as well as new possibilities in the form of 'minor liberties' (Dutta 2020) or 'little freedoms' (Hatcher 2019; also see P. Ngai 2005; Otis 2016). As such, rather than assess women's employment merely as an instrument for empowerment or neglect the enmeshing of employment in broader life-making activities, the book situates women's working lives as a site for crafting new subjectivities and a new social politics.

Making middle lives

The young women who are the central actors in this book have worked in a range of jobs in cafés, shopping malls, call centres and offices. They described themselves variously as 'middle class', 'lower middle class' or simply 'in the middle', referring to their position in between the working poor and the secure middle class. This is not to suggest a clear division between the upper and lower middle classes. Rather, the descriptor 'lower' reflects the insecurity that pervades the lives of people who may be understood to be upwardly mobile or transitioning into higher-class status, in this case, particularly through participation in the lower levels of the new service economy. In contrast to the neatness of classifications in much of the scholarship on class in the Global North, this book demonstrates the messiness of the middle class in India by using the lower middle class as a magnifying lens for the study of class formations. By focusing on lower-middle-class women, the book addresses a lacuna in the literature on women's work, which, as Samita Sen (2021) puts it, focuses on either working-class women (that is, poor women) or working women (that is, middle-class professionals).

In this book, I draw attention to the politics of *class formation* – the question is not so much exactly about *who* comprises this new middle class, or what its size is, but what the emergence of the new middle class as a category, descriptor or classification *does*. More specifically, what social relations are imbricated in the construction of the new middle class? What kinds of labour arrangements and relations of exploitation is it premised upon? The women discussed their middle-class status, but being 'in the middle' was not only about class identification. Rather, it indicated a much more complex experience of navigating life amidst rapid socio-economic change. Based on her long-term ethnographic research in Madurai, Sara Dickey (2012) reflects on what it means to be 'middle people' in the context of socio-economic change in urban south India. A position that is both desirable or pleasurable and unstable or anxious, she suggests, being in the middle is closely associated with the pressure to uphold social mores. Of course, it is women who are primarily responsible for the maintenance of propriety through the exercise of moderation, which indicates the deeply gendered nature of being 'in the middle' or 'in-between'. Women may negotiate this responsibility by developing what Gowri Vijayakumar (2013) calls 'flexible aspirations'; Vijayakumar shows that women working in a small-town business process outsourcing unit (BPO) on the outskirts of the city of Bangalore distinguish themselves from both 'old-fashioned village housewives' and 'promiscuous urban call centre girls'. They mould and change their future lives to varying circumstances at different sites. This may be informed by 'insecurity about one's place during periodic innovation, fear of losing recently gained privileges, and anxiety over being "left behind"', which may 'translate into flexibility, adaptability, and a readiness to reconfigure oneself' (Virno, quoted in S. Ngai 2004: 3–4).

'Middle-ness' speaks to the experiences of being interstitial, bound, ambivalent, ambiguous, in-flux and anxious, but it is not limited to or exhaustively explained by any of these. In part, the women expressed middle-ness through their complicated attitudes towards employment. While asserting their desire to be in paid work, particularly against the alternative of 'sitting at home' (see Chapter 3), they also recognised their duties towards the home. They not only contributed financially to their family's upkeep but also willingly and actively participated in what Hanna Papanek (1979) calls 'status-production' work, such as attending religious and social events, contributing to preparations for festivals, visiting their paternal villages, and so on. Such work often conflicted with their employment, leading to some of them quitting paid work in favour of attending to family duties (see Chapter 6). This 'in-between' positioning extended to other areas of their lives. They identified themselves as 'urban' women – not *dehaati*, or rural – and expressed this through their clothing, form of expression, English speaking, employment in new services, and so on, as detailed in Chapters 3 and 5. But they felt compelled to counteract this urban freedom with assertions of virtuosity.

The double-edged nature of their experiences is, to a certain extent, explained through the framework of boundaries or boundary-work, which is commonly used to understand class as relational and processual. It usefully captures young women's distancing from multiple positions – housewives, promiscuous professionals, rural or uneducated women, and so on. But it offers little by way of understanding the experience, meaning and implications of being in the middle. The anthropological concept of liminal or liminality then perhaps comes closest to a reading of such middle-ness. In anthropology, the term 'liminal' or 'liminality' has been variously used. The open-ended nature of the concept lends itself to multiple meanings, encompassing boundaries, marginality and interstitiality (Ghannam 2011; Silva 2016; Wels et al. 2011). For this book, which concerns itself with young women's uncertainties of life against the popular discourse of growth, development and modernity in India, marginalisation in the globalising economy, and contested subjectivities between home and work, the concept of 'liminal' has its attractions. Developed by the anthropologist Victor Turner (1967, 1969) (drawing upon the work of the anthropologist Arnold van Gennep), the 'liminal' elaborates upon the middle stage of the 'rites of passage' in kinship communities, referring to the ambiguous state of the subject 'between and betwixt', passing from one stage to the next. I find value in deploying the concept of the 'liminal' to focus on instability in subject formation. These young women's liminality, however, is not a reference to the 'essentially unstructured' that Turner attends to. It is rather an attempt to pry open that which is 'interstructural' – in other words, that which is ambiguous and ambivalent by virtue of being between structures, pushed and pulled in both directions. Further, while liminality emphasises transition, these women's experience of middle-ness is enduring.

In navigating work, home and leisure, women grapple with competing discourses of modernity, freedom, urbanity, domesticity, respectability, consumerism, mobility, and so on. But rather than reconciling these, my research shows that women sit with and draw out the tensions, contradictions and ambivalences of being in the middle. This middle-ness is therefore not simply conciliatory of two extreme positions; rather, it interrogates and challenges various positions. This culture of middle-ness does not simply 'aspire' to the dominant symbolic order of the upper classes but can be wayward, messy and disruptive. In other words, these women are not, contrary to popular imagination, aspiring to become elites. Indeed, I argue that it is precisely by playing the role of *mediating agents*, by adopting middle-ness as the framework of their lives, that women are navigating reproduction of inequalities as well as effecting social change. In that, this middle-ness is the defining structure of young, lower-middle-class women's lives.

The strategy of mid-identification

The book extends middle-ness beyond class to understand it as an expression of the way in which young women make their lives and thus as a key structure for subject formation. Drawing upon their narratives in which they engage with emerging subjectivities in relation to emerging cultures of work, I propose that their life-making is carried out through the process of mid-identification, or simultaneous identification and disidentification. I do not aim to exhaustively review the vast scholarship on identity, identification and subjectivities, so I will limit myself to the discussion of ideas that have informed and inspired my thinking. It needs to be stated foremost that the concept of mid-identification builds on the young women's narratives of middle-ness as discussed earlier. As a form of navigation, middle-ness manifests in what might at first glance seem like ambivalence in claiming subjectivities in relation to the figure of the professional woman. They are working women, but they are also not working women in the way the world might perceive working women. There is therefore a double consciousness at play; Aimee Cox (2015: 10) identifies the same among low-income Black girls and young women in a shelter in Detroit, United States. Building on an interlocutor's narrative about 'the missing middle' (also see Lemanski and Lama-Rewal 2013; Mawdsley, Mehra and Beazley 2009), she writes,

> For Janice, the missing middle is the thick, complex, richly textured, and uncategorizable aspects of the lives of young low-income Black women, and that is what constitutes their 'truth,' or their legibility as fully human. Her words convey a double consciousness that is both aware of external assumptions made about Black girls and attuned to the fact that Black girls create their own measures of success, health, and happiness.

When women engage with this double consciousness – the way they see (and want to see) themselves versus the way the world sees them – they enter a dialectic of constraint and freedom. This is precisely where Lois McNay's (2000: 9) understanding of subjectivities as involving a dual process of simultaneous 'subjectification' – that is, the constitution of the subject through subjection (Foucault 1984, 1988) and 'self-conscious stylisation' – becomes useful. Drawing upon McNay, I place narratives at the centre of understanding the self. We may highlight certain aspects in narrating our lives – the body of literature on work or worker subjectivities assigns primary importance to paid or income-generating work in the constitution of subjectivities (du Gay 1996). Here, I propose to understand subjectivities through the framework of 'working lives' – that is, in relation to the range of activities (including paid employment, unpaid work, leisure, education, and so on) that the young women undertake to make their lives.

When young women are *subjected to* identifications that contain pejorative and derogatory tones, they distance themselves through the process of 'disidentification' – that is, the process of emphasising *who they are not*. Beverley Skeggs (1997) sketches out the concept of disidentification in her pioneering work on gender and class relations, showing that when people are assigned injurious identifications, they adopt disidentification or identifying against as a strategy to preserve their sense of the self. I find that the young women in Delhi similarly reject or disidentify from certain subject positions: they are not *dehaati*; they are not housewives; they are not 'B-grade' girls. But, interestingly and crucially, there are emerging subjectivities that they both identify with and identify against. In this book, each chapter explores how these women use mid-identification as a strategy: they cherish employment for offering them an opportunity to traverse the city, but they worry about being branded 'fast-forward'; they desire to be fluent in English speaking, but they do not want to be mocked for being 'madams'; they want to dress as professionals, but they emphasise that they do not want to deceive people as 'heroines' do; they come from 'middle-class' families, but they distance themselves from 'middle class-ness' through their behaviours and attitudes, and, importantly, not through money; they are 'working', but they quit work to assert agency that is denied to working women.

Crucially, as Skeggs' work shows, and I reiterate in this book, the self, rather than being an abstract reflection of an inner or real self, is reliant on or grounded in the range of life-making activities that we engage in by virtue of our social place in the given context. I argue that mid-identification is a strategy for these young women because they are situated on the margins of and amidst the flux of socio-economic change. There is no clear boundary-making in this context because the boundaries are constantly shifting, and women are central to this pushing and changing of boundaries.

People and (dis)locations in the field

In the early days of fieldwork in August 2016 in Delhi, I started frequenting a café, not far from where I was living at the time in South Delhi. Its air-conditioned interiors provided respite from the summer heat, and its coffee and sandwiches offered a familiar comfort. On my first day in the café, one of the workers, Sheela, came up to me and said, 'Ma'am, you're very nice, come again tomorrow.' And so I did. Through my regular visits to the café, I got to know Sheela and Prachi. Sheela was the more 'senior' worker, having worked at the café for longer; Prachi had joined only recently. I found time to talk to them in the mornings, when the café was largely deserted and the manager had not yet arrived. Afternoons were busier; the café was frequented by some locals and students from a nearby Delhi University college. While Sheela had studied up to class 12 (pre-university level), Prachi was pursuing higher education via a Bachelor of Arts (BA) programme through Delhi University's School of Open Learning (SOL). Both in their early 20s, they were serving coffee, cakes and sandwiches to customers in the same age group, addressing them as 'ma'am' and 'sir'.

At that early stage of fieldwork, I thought that by situating myself in a café, I could conduct non-participant observation, eventually expanding access to workers in other cafés in South Delhi. However, this visage of ethnographic coherence was temporary. Prachi quit work a couple of months after I met her. Following her impulsive resignation, over several meetings in the food court of Select Citywalk, Prachi shared the frustrations she had felt at work, including low pay, long working hours and disrespectful treatment from the manager. She attributed the manager's condescending attitude to his judgement of her as a 'working woman' whose family sent her to work because of financial difficulties. She suggested that he expected her to 'work silently', assuming that the work was indispensable for her but that, as an employee in the café, she was dispensable. Prachi mentioned several friends who had similarly quit work in the recent past, horizontally moving from call centres to cafés to offices without a significant pay rise. This was a critical point in making decisions about location: I could either persevere with situating my study in the café, carrying out observations with the employees who came and went, or I could follow Prachi and her friends' lives, which would take me into unknown locations, or perhaps simply into the unknown.

This question of location was, of course, not merely an issue of where I would be physically based but one of determining analytical significance. While confining my research to the café (or other workplaces for that matter) may have given me insights into the dynamics of the new workplaces in urban India, it would have limited my interaction with the employees who may work there for only a short period of time. After Prachi quit work at the café, I hired her as my research assistant.[3] In this capacity, she arranged access for me to her friends' network and, at times, accompanied me for meetings too. As I came to know Prachi's friends, I found it hard to keep up with their frequent movements, from working to looking for a job to doing ad hoc work to studying to taking a break. When they were at work, they worked across cafés, shopping malls, call centres and offices of varying sizes and kinds. I met other women, besides Prachi's friends, by approaching skill centres and contacts in non-government organisations (NGOs). By deciding to follow the women, rather than situate myself in a workplace as is common and conventional for ethnographies of work (Smith 2001), I engaged with what I call ethnographic 'dislocation' or unexpected shuttling in the field (Islam 2022), gaining insights into women's working lives, including in between and beyond employment. I continued visiting workplaces when I could (mostly cafés and some offices). I got a few invitations to women's homes, but the sites that we frequented the most for our meetings were spaces of leisure: shopping malls, cafés, parks (Figure 1.1). The conversations were held primarily in Hindi, but with a smattering of English words, phrases and sentences. Some of the English words that refer to emerging subjectivities are particularly significant in the book. In direct quotes, I have highlighted the original use of English through italicisation.

The young women I conducted this research with were all at the time between 19 and 23 years of age, unmarried and living with their families in one- or two-bedroom apartments, mostly rented, although some families owned them, in the neighbourhood of Dakshinpuri (Figure 1.2). They had all completed schooling, and most were enrolled in higher education programmes through distance learning mode. Many of them had also gained training at skill centres in computers, specialised data management software and English speaking. As a young Indian woman with native fluency in Hindi, I found it relatively easy to 'gain access to' and spend time with these young women. There was, however, a wide class gap between us, which was obvious and commented upon by the women. The interlocutors used me as a reference point for 'hi-fi', or high-class, people, in contrast to themselves and others they referred to as 'middle class' or 'in the middle', highlighting their understanding of class as relational. Jahanvi called a customer who frequented the café she was working at *middle class*. When I asked her how

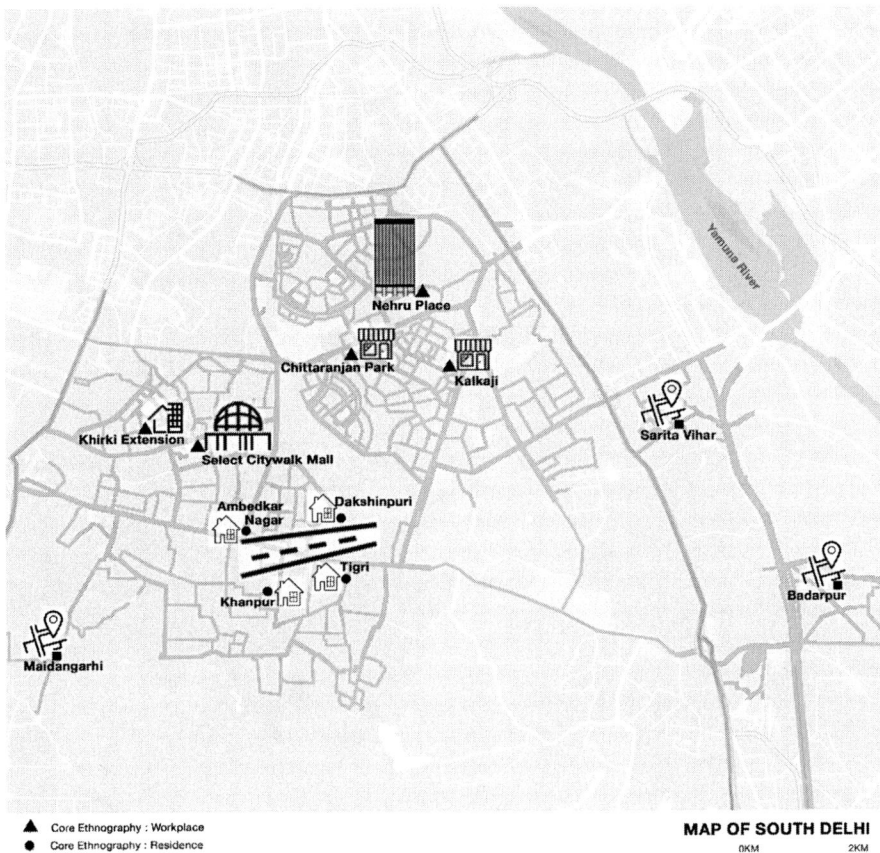

Figure 1.1 Map of South Delhi showing the main workplaces (Select Citywalk mall in Saket and cafés and offices in the neighbourhoods of Nehru Place, Chittranjan Park and Kalkaji) and residential neighbourhoods (Dakshinpuri, Khanpur, Ambedkar Nagar and Tigri) that featured in my fieldwork

Source: Map prepared by the author.

she knew he was middle class, she nonchalantly replied, 'I can tell, like with you, can't call you *middle class*, there's a difference of *personality, attitude*. I can recognise quite a lot of people.' Telling me about the first time she went out with her office colleagues and boyfriend, Chandni said she felt really *middle class* among all of them. Deepti, a café worker, specifically used the term *lower middle class* when I asked if she sees herself as middle class. She contrasted herself against her manager, who, she said, earned INR 50,000 per month, owned a car and was *proper middle class*.[4] Meeta classified her family as middle

Figure 1.2 A lane in Dakshinpuri with three-storey buildings on either side
Source: Photograph by the author.

class but asserted that their *thinking* was not middle class on account of their
support for her employment. In other words, her family may be middle class
in financial terms, but their approving attitude towards women's employment
implied transcendence from that status. Importantly, it needs to be noted that
in contrast to the desirability of middle class depicted in the research from
the Global North,[5] these women used the term 'middle class' pejoratively and
attempted to distance themselves from it.

They were cautious in asserting their ability to transcend their class status but saw their youth as potentially enabling a move away from being middle class. Age came up often as a topic of conversation between me and my interlocutors. The most common iteration of age was related to appearance: Sheela, six years younger than me, asked me how I managed to look so 'young'. Jahanvi loudly exclaimed 'Oh my god!' when she found out that I was 28 years old at the time. She thought I looked much younger; her guess was off by five years: 'I'm 21 years old…. How old are you? I think around 23.' She thought my ability to look young was admirable; it was something that was innate in her too:

> *Actually*, even with me, I do a *job* but everyone says, '*Ma'am*, did you get this *job* without checking your age?' I don't seem mature, maybe it's because of the way I behave. My face, and also the way I talk. I don't keep in mind that I'm 21, so I don't behave that way. That's what everyone says. I don't like acting my age at all; I just want to be like this throughout my life.

Jahanvi's wish to 'be like this throughout my life' – to preserve youth – is possibly near universal. But age and, indeed, appearance are also linked closely to attitudes, aspirations and achievements. Being (and looking) young implies that there are possibilities still open for the future, that indeed there is a future at all. As such, it is evident that the category 'youth' does not simply refer to an age group; instead, it is a sociocultural construction drawing upon a multitude of circulating discourses.

Although caste did not come up as explicitly as class in my discussions with the women, it was always there, under the surface. Caste was readily mentioned when the women talked about romantic relationships and marriages, being careful not to enter inter-caste relationships, knowing that they would fail under family pressures. Caste was also, at times, used as a descriptor for attitudes and behaviours. Chandni always maintained that her family, although middle class, are open-minded because they are Garhwalis.[6] Between the workers, there were clear hierarchies of class and caste; the women in this research were positioned in between their lower-middle-class and low- to middle-caste status, with managers usually coming from more securely middle-class and higher-caste backgrounds, and with cleaning work in cafés, malls and offices relegated to low-caste people (further discussed in Chapter 7). Perhaps surprisingly, religion did not feature much in our discussions. The women – all Hindu – talked about the celebration of religious festivals or the observance of religious rituals but did not enquire about my religion. They knew me by only my first name and discovered my last name (which pretty much gives away my religious background) when I asked them to sign consent forms. Some of them expressed surprise at my Muslim name but did not venture into further discussions (perhaps partly because I, as an atheist, was reticent about it).

The jobs that these women were in had embellished titles, such as 'barista', 'brew master', 'beauty assistant' and 'customer relations executive'. These frilly titles provide a front of professionalism for jobs that are largely poorly paid, with little opportunity for stability and progression, as Chapter 6 particularly shows. At the time, their salaries in these varied roles were between INR 7,000 and 12,000 per month, close to the minimum wage in Delhi. For young women, these were *jobs*, or short-term work, rather than *career*, or long-term professional engagement that yields higher material rewards. And yet a *job* was preferable over *labour-type* work, or manual work, which some of their parents did, and *ghar ka kaam*, or housework. In rejecting labour-type work and housework, women made assertions about the type of work that was appropriate for them on the basis of their higher educational levels. The use of these varied terms for work finds resonance in Jonathan Parry's (2013) analysis of how workers in a public-sector Indian steel plant differentiated between *naukri* as secure employment and *kaam* as insecure wage labour, resulting in social distinctions between the two groups. Hannah Arendt identifies 'labour' and 'work' as distinct categories on the simple basis that most European languages contain different terms for these seemingly similar activities. Through their historical and contemporary usage and reliance on a Marxist understanding, Arendt (1998 [1958]: 7) proposes that labour is natural while work is artifice: 'The human condition of labour is life itself.' I argue that in referring to their employment as 'jobs' rather than 'careers', the young women participated in paid work not as a discrete form of labour but as one of many labours to build and secure their lives.

This meandering ethnography, then, engaged with women's working lives as they negotiated and renegotiated the entanglements of gender, class and caste through their participation in the new service economy. The predominant form of the ethnography between August 2016 and June 2017 was informal conversations, mostly long discussions when we spent time together eating in food courts of malls, visiting parks, hanging out at their homes or in their workplaces, and sometimes exchanging snippets on

WhatsApp. In the final months of my fieldwork, I conducted semi-structured interviews with the women, lasting an hour on average, focusing on their work trajectories. In addition, I visited neighbourhood skill centres, met managers and trainers and talked to students enrolled in short-term courses there. I also spoke to unemployed women and young girls in Dakshinpuri. At the heart of it, I was and continue to be interested in how women narrated their lives – their past, their present and their future – themselves. The way we tell our life-stories is deeply embedded in the sense we have of our place in the world. But this place is not static; it is constantly shifting and evolving and may be particularly volatile for those who are marginalised in processes of globalisation and development.

While the fieldwork officially concluded in June 2017, I have retained contact through WhatsApp with some of the women who contributed to my research, learning about their successes and failures at finding work, frustrations with the work they were doing, plans to study, family problems, and so on. Over the years, I have met them every time I have visited Delhi – too many visits to be listed here, but usually once or twice a year since 2017. Admittedly, I have not devised a systematic way of recording these informal conversations, in part because such recording feels intrusive given the evolution of our relationship beyond my research and in part because such recording may break the natural flow of the conversation. Instead, I have relied on my researcher's sense of listening to and understanding the women's perspectives. During that time, several things changed for me: I completed my PhD, did a postdoc and secured a lectureship. For the women, things moved much more slowly: in 2017–18, it seemed like they were mostly unable to progress in their jobs as well as unable to find work they liked. They have all done a variety of jobs over the years, many of them having moved recently into desk-based work – data entry, backend work, logistics – in emerging start-ups of various kinds. The lives of these young women reflect and engage with ongoing transformations of work in urban India.

The structure of the book

The case for middling concepts

In using 'mid-identification' as the framework through which to understand young women's lives, I am making a case for middling concepts (drawing inspiration from thick or thin concepts [Abend 2019]). I understand mid-identification as a middling concept in two ways. As a concept that is meant to help us understand how young people may navigate their lives amidst socio-economic change, it does not explain *everything*. In that, it is a partial concept – it contributes towards understanding various aspects of young women's everyday lives, but it does not necessarily speak to *all* aspects of their lives. In other words, middle-ness may be the dominant structuring framework of their lives, but it does not necessarily explain their lives in their entirety. Middle-ness is also a middling concept because, rather than explaining away, it engages with messiness, ambivalence and waywardness of people's lives. In embracing partiality of knowledge and complexity of lives, the concept of middle-ness is inspired by feminist research praxis.

The processes of seeking and producing knowledge are intrinsically imbued with power relations – feminist scholars have long challenged the definitions of and boundaries between the knower (the researcher) and the to-be-known (the researched) in the field (Abu-Lughod 1990; Alcoff 1992; Oakley 1981). They have also questioned the quest for *complete* knowledge, demonstrated in, for example, ideal constructions of ethnographic fieldwork as research in which the researcher is fully immersed in and emerges with exhaustive knowledge about the field. Indeed, such an ideal construction is based upon a normative academic subject and settings – 'a world that all the time stays in place and is wandered across, mapped, extracted from and calibrated by privileged groups of men' (Gunaratnam and Hamilton 2017: 2). It is then perhaps my or our own partial belonging that also invites reflection on and engagement with the messiness of people's lives, rather than a quest to grant them coherence. Saidiya Hartman's *Wayward Lives, Beautiful Experiments* (2019) does this beautifully with reference to Black women's lives in early-20th-century Philadelphia and New York through the concept of the 'wayward':

> Wayward: the unregulated movement of drifting and wandering; sojourns without a fixed destination, ambulatory possibility, interminable migrations, rush and flight, black locomotion; the everyday struggle to live free. The attempt to elude capture by never settling…. Waywardness articulates the paradox of cramped creation, the entanglement of space and confinement, flight and captivity.

It is significant that waywardness as the mode of life is the concept that explains their lives rather than another meta-concept that explains away waywardness. It is this inspiring scholarship that I follow by proposing mid-identification as a middling concept that emerges through young women's reflections on their own lives. By thinking through, rather than against, middle-ness, I invite the readers to stay with the messiness, ambivalence and uncertainty that characterise young women's lives.

The social life of things

This book features Delhi's young women in various settings – in their residential neighbourhoods, in their workplaces, in spaces of leisure, such as malls, cafés and parks. We meet their friends, families and colleagues as we encounter some of the sights, sounds and feel of these spaces, ranging from the traffic passing by streetside food stalls to music playing in the food court of a shopping mall. In this course, we also encounter *things*; these are things that are significant in young women's lives. These are things that they either already have access to or desire access to in order to signal 'distinction'. Importantly, they are things that are in circulation in the popular discourse of globalisation: smartphones, burgers, jeans, credit cards and, of course, malls. As such, these things connect the minutiae of women's everyday lives to the larger picture of socio-economic transformation in urban India and development and globalisation in the Global South more generally. Further, contestations over these objects reveal the middle-ness of young women's lives.

In engaging with these things, I am inspired by Arjun Appadurai's (1986) conceptualisation of 'the social life of things'. Although Appadurai's treatise on objects, value and social relations is based on art objects, I extend it to the analysis of everyday things with the understanding that these things make up our lives and connect us to the larger world. In that sense, these commodities are useful not just for examining relationships between labour and capital but also, more intricately, where we are placed in the world.

Chapter sequence

Each chapter of the book opens with an ethnographic vignette that introduces one character, one thing and one emerging subjectivity that women mid-identify with; other characters and more things appear during the course of the chapter. The sequence of the chapters follows a loose temporality of women's entry into (Chapters 2 and 3), experiences of (Chapters 4 and 5) and exit (Chapter 6) from paid work, drawing to a close with a discussion of the conditions that structure women's longer-term futures (Chapter 7). While women's employment provides a reference point to understand the constitution of youth, gender, class and caste relations, the chapters position it very much with reference to the wider framework of life-making.

The economic restructuring of the early 1990s offers an imagination of a 'new' India, where rags-to-riches mobility is possible through a happy marriage of youth aspirations and economic opportunities. Chapter 2 begins with a discussion of how young women's efforts to enter the world of service employment are characterised by struggle (which they refer to as *tensions*) against their constrained access to the resources that can enable it. One such resource is the English language, which this chapter analyses with reference to the figure of *madam* or *ma'am*. Having gone to Hindi-medium government schools, these young women are not already fluent English speakers, as young people who come from secure middle- or upper-class backgrounds with access to English-medium private schools are. They enrol in short-term courses to learn the English language to be successful at job interviews, in work training and, of course, in their workplaces. While 'ma'am' is a term of respectful address they use for customers and managers, their capability to speak English offers them the possibility of becoming 'ma'am' themselves. But this possibility is tenuous – unable to gain fluency in the language, they resort to using it only strategically for purposes of employment and deploy the term 'madam' to mock their peers who speak in English outside of the workplace. The chapter shows the discrepancy between the popular discourse and the lived realities of 'middle class', leading to the duality of the subjective position of madam or ma'am.

Chapter 3 discusses that to enter work, young women proactively shun domesticity, classifying it as 'boring', and assert that employment is or should be a natural consequence of their education. Upending common understandings of time and work-discipline under capitalism, they position time at work as their 'own' time and time spent on reproductive activities at home as communal time. They learn how to navigate the metropolis to (quite literally) reach spaces of work – buses are cheap and crowded, the air-conditioned metro is preferable but expensive, autorickshaws are essential for last-mile connectivity. Through employment, then, young women are able to create possibilities of leisure for themselves – not only does work provide them a legitimate reason to be away from home, it also familiarises them with the city. However, this mobility – while desirable and pleasurable – has to be carefully managed since too much of it can lead to the stamp of being *fast-forward*.

Besides physical mobility, their jobs afford them access to personal consumption that they can indulge in without the knowledge and/or intervention of their families. While critically reflecting on the constraints of their lives, young women tentatively attempt to access the promised upward mobility through consumer culture in Delhi. Although a large chunk of their income goes towards the maintenance of families, young women are able to claim, whether overtly or covertly, some part of their salary for personal expenses. Strikingly, the expenses they incur with their 'own' money are expenses their parents do not have experience with and, in many cases, would not approve of. For example, while the previous generation may think smartphones are a wasteful expenditure, young women know their uses and their pleasures in the modern world. But they also assert that their consumption is moderate; they emphasise that they primarily work for the welfare of their families and criticise women who use all or a significant part of their income for personal consumption. Navigating the crossroads of transformations in the roles of breadwinners and consumers alike, they situate themselves in the middle of 'middle class' and 'not middle class'. *Middle class*, as Chapter 4 explores, is a label that these women use both as a form of identification and for the practice of distantiation.

Building on the discussion of consumption in the previous chapter, Chapter 5 examines the boundaries between propriety and impropriety that young women have to navigate through their bodies. Modelling themselves as service professionals through make-up, clothing and body language is both a prerequisite to and a consequence of their entry into the new economy. They express a liking for jeans – a ubiquitous symbol of global belonging – in opposition to 'traditional' clothing. As such, for young women, these makeovers, enabled by and through employment, are a mechanism of pleasure. But they are a cause for anxiety too – while cultivating urban sophistication at work, they have to simultaneously dissociate themselves from urban promiscuity. Their appearance is, as such, a site of the making and unmaking of class and gender relations, which young women navigate by asserting not only the respectability but also the virtuosity of their professionalism. Chapter 5 explores the trope of *heroine*, which, similar to 'madam', is a figure of both aspiration and shame. A 'heroine' can be flamboyant and fun, but she is also an actor, pretending to be someone she is not.

Chapter 6 reflects on *working* as a gendered identity by exploring moments of refusal and resistance in young women's working lives. These moments of refusal emerge in young women's transition from one activity into another as they try to find middle ground between work and home, between professionalism and respectability and between necessity and aspiration. Their outbursts at work – following an argument with a manager or a colleague – are expressed through their will to impulsively write resignation letters. Women may leave employment, even if only temporarily, to assert their agency and protest precarious working conditions. They are and want to be 'working', but not at the cost of relentless exploitation. This 'resignation' is to be found in other arenas of their lives too, as previous chapters show. They may similarly leave a skill training course without completing it, recognising that its success as a strategy for improving their opportunities is limited. They may also resist marriage and motherhood by pointing to examples where these have failed to afford stability to women. Through such refusal, young women generate middle spaces, whereby moments of transition, rather than transition in itself, are significant for life-making.

Chapter 7 opens with a set of conversations I conducted with unemployed women and young school-going girls in Dakshinpuri. Younger than the interlocutors for this research, the school-going girls reiterate the desire for education and employment. Using these conversations, this chapter delves into the gendered aspects of partial investment in education and employment and partial disinvestment from marriage and family that underpin the negotiation of subjectivities that I conceptualise as mid-identification. These emerging subjectivities, rather than merely describing the inclinations of young lower-middle-class women in Delhi, point towards reconfiguration of gender, class and caste relations in urban India. Through a discussion of a changing sense of the self, the chapter reiterates the importance of analysing middle-ness as an enduring condition of life for those marginalised in globalising economies.

Notes

1. The statistics on women's participation in the workforce paint a dismal picture, although they need to be treated with caution because of the complexities of accounting for women's work (Neetha 2014; Sudarshan and Bhattacharya 2009). The Periodic Labour Force Survey's annual report of 2022–23 (Ministry

of Statistics and Programme Implementation 2023) notes that only 30.5 per cent of rural women and 20.2 per cent of urban women are in the workforce.

2. According to the 2022–23 annual report of the Periodic Labour Force Survey, the highest proportion of urban female workers, at 40.1 per cent, is in 'other services'. The category 'other services' refers to a wide range of activities, including (paid) domestic work, which is where a large proportion of women would have been concentrated, as well as the work that the women who feature in this book did in malls, call centres, cafés and offices. In comparison, only 20.6 per cent of urban male workers were in 'other services' for the same time period.

3. Recruiting Prachi, who was initially my 'interlocutor', as my research assistant made me reflect on who can (or cannot) assume the role of the 'research assistant' in the field and what the role entails. The relationship with Prachi, although formalised through a contract that set out her pay and terms and conditions of work, remained largely informal, with Prachi insisting that she was happy to go out of her way to 'help' me. I have since also grappled with the issue of anonymisation. Prachi features in my work in both her capacities – as an interlocutor and as a research assistant. While I promised her anonymity for her former role, she rightly wanted recognition for her latter. I have used her pseudonym throughout to convey how the research assistant arrangement came about, but I have provided her a 'certificate of experience' in her actual name to use with her CV for job applications.

4. At the time of writing, INR 80 and INR 100 equalled to USD 1 and GBP 1, respectively.

5. While the women used various terms for their class status – 'middle', 'middle class', 'lower middle class', 'not high class', 'not hi-fi', and so on – they were consistent in their assessment of 'middle class' as an undesirable position. That is, they were not seeking mobility to the middle class but saw themselves as already middle class, and they did not want to be middle class. This is in contrast to research from the Global North that highlights women's desire to become middle class (Lawler 1999; Skeggs 1997). This may, in part, be attributed to the use of 'Hinglish' – a mix of Hindi and English – whereby certain English terms come to acquire related but new understandings (on the language of class, see Phadi and Manda 2010). This is not to assert that middle-class status is repudiated across India. Indeed, it may be that the meaning of middle class changes in different regions as the term comes into interaction with other Indian languages.

6. Garhwali is a regional, ethnic and linguistic identity. Interestingly, in this context, Chandni used it to explain that different castes display different class

behaviours: '*Middle class* status … it's just that castes like *Baniya* or mine, *Garhwali*, they have a lot of money, but they'll show that they don't. They'll go and look around in other people's houses. If somebody has boys over, they'll ask why are boys here. We're going to office, *of course*, we know boys.… *High class* are those who might not have much money but they have good thinking.'

References

Abend, Gabriel. 2019. 'Thick Concepts and Sociological Research'. *Sociological Theory* 37(3): 209–33. DOI: 10.1177/0735275119869979.

Abraham, Vinoj. 2013. 'Missing Labour or Consistent "De-Feminisation"?' *Economic and Political Weekly* 48(31): 99–108.

Abu-Lughod, Lila. 1990. 'Can There Be a Feminist Ethnography?' *Women and Performance* 5.1(9): 7–27. DOI: 10.1080/07407709008571138.

Alcoff, Linda. 1992. 'The Problem of Speaking for Others'. *Cultural Critique* 20(20): 5–32.

Appadurai, Arjun. 1986. 'Introduction: Commodities and the Politics of Value'. In *The Social Life of Things: Commodities in Cultural Perspective*, edited by Arjun Appadurai, 3–63. Cambridge, UK: Cambridge University Press.

Arendt, Hannah. 1998 (1958). *The Human Condition*. Chicago, IL: University of Chicago Press.

Aslany, Maryam. 2019. 'The Indian Middle Class, Its Size, and Urban-Rural Variations'. *Contemporary South Asia* 27(2): 196–213. DOI: 10.1080/09584935.2019.1581727.

Baas, Michiel. 2020. *Muscular India: Masculinity, Mobility and the New Middle Class*. Chennai: Context Publications.

Banerjee, Abhijit V., and Esther Duflo. 2008. 'What Is Middle Class about the Middle Classes around the World?' *Journal of Economic Perspectives* 22 (December): 3–28.

Banerjee, Nirmala. 1990. 'Working Women in Colonial Bengal: Modernization and Marginalization'. In *Recasting Women: Essays in Indian Colonial History*, edited by Kumkum Sangari and Sudesh Vaid, 269–301. New Brunswick, NJ: Rutgers University Press.

Belliappa, Jyothsna Latha. 2013. *Gender, Class and Reflexive Modernity in India*. Hampshire: Palgrave Macmillan.

Bhattacharya, Gargi. 2018. *Rethinking Racial Capitalism: Questions of Reproduction and Survival*. London: Rowman & Littlefield Publishers.

Bhattacharya, Tithi (ed.). 2017. *Social Reproduction Theory: Remapping Class, Recentering Oppression*. London: Pluto Press.

Bourdieu, Pierre. 2010 (1984). *Distinction: A Social Critique of the Judgement of Taste*. Abingdon, Oxon: Routledge.

Cox, Aimee Meredith. 2015. *Shapeshifters: Black Girls and the Choreography of Citizenship*. Durham, NC: Duke University Press.

Dattatreyan, Ethiraj Gabriel. 2020. *The Globally Familiar: Digital Hip Hop, Masculinity, and Urban Space in Delhi*. Durham, NC: Duke University Press.

Dhawan, Nandita Banerjee. 2010. 'The Married "New Indian Woman": Hegemonic Aspirations in New Middle-Class Politics?' *South African Review of Sociology* 41(3): 45–60. DOI: 10.1080/21528586.2010.516122.

Dickey, Sara. 2012. 'The Pleasures and Anxieties of Being in the Middle: Emerging Middle-Class Identities in Urban South India'. *Modern Asian Studies* 46(3): 559–99.

Dutta, Madhumita. 2020. 'Workplace, Emotional Bonds and Agency: Everyday Gendered Experiences of Work in an Export Processing Zone in Tamil Nadu, India'. *Environment and Planning A: Economy and Space* 52(7): 1357–74. DOI: 10.1177/0308518X20904076.

Evans, Mary. 2020. *Making Respectable Women: Changing Moralities, Changing Times*. London: Palgrave Macmillan.

Federici, Silvia. 2009. 'The Reproduction of Labour-Power in the Global Economy, Marxist Theory and the Unfinished Feminist Revolution'. Seminar on 'Crisis of Social Reproduction and Feminist Struggle', UC Santa Cruz, CA, 27 January.

———. 2012 (1975). 'Wages against Housework'. *The Commoner* 15. Originally published jointly by Falling Wall Press and the Power of Women Collective.

Fernandes, Leela. 2000. 'Restructuring the New Middle Class in Liberalizing India'. *Comparative Studies of South Asia, Africa and the Middle East* 20(1–2): 88–112. DOI: 10.1215/1089201X-20-1-2-88.

———. 2006. *India's New Middle Class: Democratic Politics in an Era of Economic Reform*. Minneapolis (MN) and London: University of Minnesota Press.

Foucault, Michel. 1984. 'The Ethic of Care for the Self as a Practice of Freedom'. *Philosophy and Social Criticism* 12(2–3): 112–32.

———. 1988. 'Technologies of the Self'. In *Technologies of the Self: A Seminar with Michel Foucault*, edited by Luther H. Martin, Huck Gutman and Patrick H. Hutton, 16–49. London: University of Massachusets Press/ Tavistock Publications. Ganguly-Scrase, Ruchira. 2003. 'Paradoxes of Globalization, Liberalization, and Gender Equality: The Worldviews of the Lower Middle Class in West Bengal, India'. *Gender and Society* 17(4): 544–66.

Ganguly-Scrase, Ruchira, and Timothy J. Scrase. 2009. *Globalisation and the Middle Classes in India: The Social and Cultural Impact of Neoliberal Reforms*. Oxford: Routledge.

du Gay, Paul. 1996. *Consumption and Identity at Work*. London: Sage Publications.

Ghannam, Farha. 2011. 'Mobility, Liminality, and Embodiment in Urban Egypt'. *American Ethnologist* 38(4): 790–800. DOI: 10.1111/j.1548-1425.2011.01337.x.

Gibson-Graham, J. K. 2008. 'Diverse Economies: Performative Practices for "Other Worlds"'. *Progress in Human Geography* 32(5): 613–32. DOI: 10.1177/0309132508090821.

Gooptu, Nandini. 2013. 'Servile Sentinels of the City: Private Security Guards, Organized Informality, and Labour in Interactive Services in Globalized India'. *International Review of Social History* 58(1): 9–38. DOI: 10.1017/S0020859012000788.

Gunaratnam, Yasmin, and Carrie Hamilton. 2017. 'Introduction: The Wherewithal of Feminist Methods'. *Feminist Review* 115(1): 1–12. DOI: 10.1057/s41305-017-0023-5.

Hartman, Saidiya. 2019. *Wayward Lives, Beautiful Experiments: Intimate Histories of Social Upheaval*. New York, NY: W. W. Norton & Company.

Hatcher, Jessamyn. 2019. '"Little Freedoms": Immigrant Labor and the Politics of "Fast Fashion" after Rana Plaza'. In *Fashion and Beauty in the Time of Asia*, edited by S. Heijin Lee, Christina H. Moon and Thuy Linh Nguyen Tu 209–41. New York, NY: NYU Press.

hooks, bell. 1984. *Feminist Theory: From Margin to Center*. Boston, MA: South End Press.

Islam, Asiya. 2022. 'Ethnographic (Dis) Locations: An Approach for Studying Marginalisation in the Context of Socio-Economic Change'. *Ethnography* 25(1): 38–57. DOI: 10.1177/14661381211058356.

Jeffrey, Craig. 2010. *Timepass: Youth, Class, and the Politics of Waiting in India*. Redwood City, CA: Stanford University Press.

John, Mary E. 2019. 'Sexual Violence 2012-2018 and #MeToo: A Touchstone for the Present'. *India Forum*, 15 April.

John, Mary E., and Meena Gopal (eds.). 2021. *Women in the Worlds of Labour: Interdisciplinary and Intersectional Perspectives*. New Delhi: Orient Blackswan.

Johri, Rachana, and Krishna Menon. 2014. 'Daily Border Crossings: Negotiations of Gender, Body and Subjectivity in the Lives of Women Workers in Urban Malls'. *Cultural Encounters, Conflicts, and Resolutions* 1(1): 1–24.

Kapsos, Steven, Andrea Silberman and Evangelia Bourmpoula. 2014. 'Why Is Female Labour Force Participation Declining So Sharply in India?' ILO Research Paper No. 10, International Labour Office, Geneva, July. https://webapps.ilo.org/wcmsp5/groups/public/---dgreports/---inst/documents/publication/wcms_250977.pdf. Accessed 21 May 2024.

Krishnan, Sneha. 2022. 'Scooty Girls Are Safe Girls: Risk, Respectability and Brand Assemblages in Urban India'. *Social and Cultural Geography* 23(3): 424–42. DOI: 10.1080/14649365.2020.1744705.

Lau, Lisa. 2010. 'Literary Representations of the "New Indian Woman": The Single, Working, Urban, Middle Class Indian Woman Seeking Personal Autonomy'. *Journal of South Asian Development* 5(2): 271–92. DOI: 10.1177/097317411000500204.

Lawler, Stephanie. 1999. '"Getting Out and Getting Away": Women's Narratives of Class Mobility'. *Feminist Economics* 63(1): 3–24.

Lemanski, Charlotte, and Stéphanie Tawa Lama-Rewal. 2013. 'The "Missing Middle": Class and Urban Governance in Delhi's Unauthorised Colonies'. *Transactions of the Institute of British Geographers* 38(1): 91–105.

Lukose, Ritty. 2009. *Liberalization's Children: Gender, Youth, and Consumer Citizenship in Globalizing India*. Durham, NC: Duke University Press.

Mawdsley, Emma, Deepshikha Mehra and Kim Beazley. 2009. 'Nature Lovers, Picnickers and Bourgeois Environmentalism'. *Economic and Political Weekly* 44(11): 49–53.

Mazumdar, Indrani. 2007. *Women Workers and Globalization: Emergent Contradictions in India*. Kolkata: Stree Samya.

McNay, Lois. 2000. *Gender and Agency*. Cambridge, UK: Polity Press.

Mezzadri, Alessandra. 2019. 'On the Value of Social Reproduction'. *Radical Philosophy* 204 (Spring): 33–41.

Ministry of Statistics and Programme Implementation. 2019. *Periodic Labour Force Survey (PLFS) Annual Report*. New Delhi: Ministry of Statistics and Programme Implementation, Government of India.

———. 2023. *Periodic Labour Force Survey Annual Report (July 2022–June 2023)*. New Delhi: Ministry of Statistics and Programme Implementation, Government of India.

Mohanty, Chandra Talpade. 1997. 'Women Workers and Capitalist Scripts: Ideologies of Domination, Common Interests, and the Politics of Solidarity'. In *Feminist Genealogies, Colonial Legacies, Democratic Futures*, edited by J. M. Alexander and C. T. Mohanty, 3–29. London and New York (NY): Routledge.

Monteith, William, Dora-Olivia Vicol and Philippa Williams (eds.). 2021. *Beyond the Wage: Ordinary Work in Diverse Economies*. Bristol: Bristol University Press.

Neetha, N. 2014. 'Crisis in Female Employment'. *Economic and Political Weekly* 49(47): 50–59.

Ngai, Pun. 2005. *Made in China: Women Factory Workers in a Global Workplace*. Durham (NC) and London: Duke University Press.

Ngai, Sianne. 2004. *Ugly Feelings*. Cambridge, MA: Harvard University Press.

Oakley, Anne. 1981. 'Interviewing Woman'. In *Doing Feminist Research*, edited by H. Roberts, 30–61. London: Routledge & Kegan Paul.

Otis, Eileen. 2016. 'China's Beauty Proletariat: The Body Politics of Hegemony in a Walmart Cosmetics Department'. *Positions* 24(1): 155–77. DOI: 10.1215/10679847-3320089.

Oza, Rupal. 2006. 'The New Liberal Indian Woman and Globalization'. In *The Making of Neoliberal India: Nationalism, Gender, and the Paradoxes of Globalization*, 21–44. New York, NY: Routledge.

Papanek, Hanna. 1979. 'Family Status Production: The "Work" and "Non-Work" of Women'. *Signs: Journal of Women in Culture and Society* 4(4): 775–81.

Parry, Jonathan. 2013. 'Company and Contract Labour in a Central Indian Steel Plant'. *Economy and Society* 42(3): 348–74. DOI: 10.1080/03085147.2013.772761.

Patel, Reena. 2010. *Working the Night Shift: Women in India's Call Center Industry*. Redwood City, CA: Stanford University Press.

Phadi, Mosa, and Owen Manda. 2010. 'The Language of Class: Southern Sotho and Zulu Meanings of "Middle Class" in Soweto'. *South African Review of Sociology* 41(3): 81–98. DOI: 10.1080/21528586.2010.516127.

Philip, Shannon. 2022. *Becoming Young Men in a New India: Masculinities, Gender Relations and Violence in the Postcolony*. New Delhi: Cambridge University Press.

Radhakrishnan, Smitha. 2011. 'Gender, the IT Revolution and the Making of a Middle-Class India'. In *Elite and Everyman: The Cultural Politics of the Indian Middle Classes*, edited by Amita Baviskar, Raka Ray, 193–219. New Delhi: Routledge.

———. 2021. *Making Women Pay: Microfinance in Urban India*. Durham, NC: Duke University Press.

Raveendran, Govindan. 2016. 'The Indian Labour Market: A Gender Perspective'. Discussion Paper No. 8, UN Women, 17 February. DOI: 10.18356/051b4d3b-en.

Raychowdhry, Poulami. 2013. '"The Delhi Gang Rape": The Making of International Causes'. *Feminist Studies* 1(39): 282–92.

Sadana, Rashmi. 2010. 'On the Delhi Metro: An Ethnographic View'. *Economic and Political Weekly* 45(46): 77–83.

Scully, Ben. 2016. 'From the Shop Floor to the Kitchen Table: The Shifting Centre of Precarious Workers' Politics in South Africa'. *Review of African Political Economy* 43(148): 295–311. DOI: 10.1080/03056244.2015.1085378.

Sen, Samita. 2021. 'Rethinking Gender and Class: Some Critical Questions for the Present'. In *Women in the Worlds of Labour: Interdisciplinary and Intersectional Perspectives*, edited by M. E. John and M. Gopal, 31–56. New Delhi: Orient Blackswan.

Silva, Elizabeth B. 2016. 'Unity and Fragmentation of the Habitus'. *Sociological Review* 64(1): 166–83. DOI: 10.1111/1467-954X.12346.

Skeggs, Beverley. 1997. *Formations of Class and Gender: Becoming Respectable*. London: Sage Publications.

Smith, Vicki. 2001. 'Ethnographies of Work and the Work of Ethnographers'. In *Handbook of Ethnography*, edited by Paul Atkinson, Amanda Coffey, Sara Delamont, John Lofland and Lyn Lofland, 220–33. London: Sage Publications Ltd.

Sudarshan, Ratna M., and Shrayana Bhattacharya. 2009. 'Through the Magnifying Glass: Women's Work and Labour Force Participation in Urban Delhi'. *Economic and Political Weekly* 44(48): 59–66. DOI: 10.2307/25663838.

Turner, Victor. 1967. 'Betwixt and Between: The Liminal Period in Rites de Passage'. In *The Forest of Symbols: Aspects of Ndembu Ritual*, by Victor Turner, 93–111. Ithaca (NY) and London: Cornell University Press.

———. 1969. 'Liminality and Communitas'. In *The Ritual Process: Structure and Anti-Structure*, by Victor Turner, 94–130 (Abridged). Chicago, IL: Aldine Publishing.

Upadhya, Carol. 2011. 'Software and "New" Middle Class in the "New India"'. In *Elite and Everyman: The Cultural Politics of the Indian Middle Classes*, edited by Amita Baviskar, Raka Ray, 166–92. New Delhi: Routledge.

Vijayakumar, Gowri. 2013. '"I'll Be Like Water"'. *Gender and Society* 27(6): 777–98. DOI: 10.1177/0891243213499445.

Wels, Harry, Kees van der Waal, Andrew Spiegel and Frans Kamsteeg. 2011. 'Victor Turner and Liminality: An Introduction'. *Anthropology Southern Africa* 34(1–2): 1–4. DOI: 10.1080/23323256.2011.11500002.

2

Madam | English

Madam/Ma'am

Prachi is perhaps the only person I know who talks about *The Merchant of Venice* and *The Three Mistakes of My Life* with equal enthusiasm. A literary masterpiece by Shakespeare and a popular novel by an Indian author, Chetan Bhagat, respectively, *The Merchant of Venice* and *The Three Mistakes of My Life* are unlikely bedfellows, but for Prachi, they have both served the same purpose – that of improving her English-language skills. Prachi's education was at a Hindi-medium government school. She tried to mitigate the disadvantage of not having learnt English from an early age by cultivating a reading habit as well as practising spoken English:

> I really like reading *novels*. You know, everyone says, the kind of *locality* I'm from and the kind of school I've studied in – I went to a *government school* – everyone says, it doesn't seem like that. I mean, my spoken English is good. Everyone asks me where I learnt English, but I never went for classes. I've never even gone for *tuitions*; it's all so expensive.

I first met Prachi in mid-2016 when I walked into a café to seek solace in its air-conditioned interiors from the heat and humidity of August in Delhi. Prachi greeted me with 'Good morning, ma'am' and a big smile – the title 'ma'am' stuck to me thereafter, with all interlocutors addressing me as such. The café was not exactly buzzing in the mornings – the crowd from the nearby Delhi University college only showed up after mid-day, and the manager was also happy letting Prachi and her colleagues manage the opening of the café at 9 a.m., joining them in the afternoon.

Over several mornings in the café, then, Prachi and I bonded over food, fiction and feminism. Prachi liked to talk in English, especially when I was around: 'I can practice with you, I don't have much opportunity otherwise.' For this, she was often mocked by her friends. Sheela, a colleague who eventually became her friend, would taunt her: '*Madam*, don't be such an *angrez*' (Don't be so English). Sheela also pointed out that 'Even *ma'am* speaks in Hindi to us', referring to my conversations with them, peppered with the suggestion, sometimes implicit, sometimes explicit, that even a UK-based Indian woman speaks Hindi, while Prachi chose to put on a show of her English skills. Prachi usually retorted by speaking in a rural dialect of Hindi, or in *dehaati*, to show that despite her ambition to be fluent in English, she had not forgotten her roots.

The distinction between 'ma'am' – the address they used for me, customers in the café and their managers – and 'madam' was pronounced. Of course, 'ma'am' is only a shortened version of 'madam', used to refer to an upper-class, upper-caste, English-speaking, professional woman, but the connotations are different. While the former was a marker of respect, work hierarchies and class hierarchies, the latter took on a mocking and, at times, even disparaging tone. Interestingly, the term 'madam', besides being a somewhat stiff and polite British address for women, has also been used to refer to women who may act as agents for sex workers or as brothel keepers. As the female equivalent for 'pimp', 'madam' is, as such, imbued with sexual politics. This sexual politics, I suggest, is related to the public and professional presence of women, which threatens social order (further discussed in Chapter 3). The significance of the mocking address 'madam' is embedded in such usage of the term, although it takes on a much broader meaning too. In mocking Prachi for her attempts to speak English, Sheela called her out for speaking in a language that did not come naturally to her but that demonstrated a certain aspiration for belonging in the global economy. It is telling that Prachi defended herself by talking in a rural dialect, showing her capability to adapt to different settings as needed. In the argument between Prachi and Sheela, it became apparent that one is a 'madam' for trying to transcend her social background, thus portending social disorder.

Although they mocked her, Prachi's friends were alert to the need for English fluency in today's world, particularly if one wants to become a 'professional' worker; at times, Sheela even admitted to envying Prachi's entrepreneurial approach to learning English. In workplaces, interviews were conducted in English, although to varying degrees. Some employers asked them to read out their résumés and talk about themselves; others had longer conversations in English to test their ability to converse with customers. In call centres, workers have to speak on the phone in English; in cafés and shopping malls, customers are greeted and assisted in English; in offices, employees are aware that English is necessary to progress.

Interestingly, women also assessed workplaces by the extent to which they actually used English. Sharing one of her many interview experiences, Chandni told me, 'My interview [for a café job] was all in English; they asked about previous six months experience. Then they slowly switched to Hindi, asked about salary expectations and working hours.' In another conversation with me, picking up on this discussion, Prachi suggested that this shift from English to Hindi revealed the reality of their workplaces: 'Chandni also said it's so *professional* in the training, neighbours think we're going to good job, then we go back to our *aukat* [status].... On the job, nobody even speaks English.'

In other words, while employers expected workers to be equipped with English fluency, this mirage of 'professionalism' was not necessarily reflected in their workplace environments. Aware of this discrepancy, young women did not necessarily aspire to become English-speaking global subjects, as is often assumed; instead, they thought this was a position not available or accessible to them and that English learning and speaking should largely be strategic rather than heartfelt, as it seemed to be in Prachi's case.

Prachi's access to school, she shared, had come at the cost of her elder sister's sacrifices; by dropping out of school and consigning herself to low-paid work as a helper in a boutique, Anamika had made her younger sibling's education possible. This arrangement came about with the understanding that through education, the younger members of the family would eventually be able to avail better employment. Yet Prachi found herself only able to secure low-paid employment in a café, leading her to reflect on how while education promises dividends, it does not necessarily pay. Craig Jeffrey, Roger Jeffery and Patricia Jeffery (2004) discuss how formal education fails to translate into respectable employment for young Dalit or low-caste men in rural Uttar Pradesh, creating a 'reproductive crisis' that manifests in the culture of 'masculine Dalit resentment'. The young women in Delhi recognised that formal education, expanding its reach among marginalised populations, is in itself not enough to secure employment in the competitive service economy. In addition to education, they therefore sought training at skill centres, enrolling in short-term courses in English, computers, customer management, and so on. Although Prachi had not pursued this route herself, her younger sister, Priya, had enrolled at a skill centre. While she secured work in the service economy, like many other young people, she found herself stuck in low-end and low-paid employment. For young women, as I will go on to show in this book and specifically in Chapter 6, progression opportunities were limited.

A good student at school, Prachi had long imagined an alternative life for herself, one in which she would work in the media industry, doing 'creative' work, rather than in a café. But this ambition, she realised, was near to impossible, even though, over the years, she had completed undergraduate and postgraduate degrees, surpassing not only her parents' but also her siblings' educational qualifications. Prachi earned these degrees through distance learning; while this allowed her to work full time for most of the time, she regretted not having had the opportunity to be a 'proper' student who would go to university campus for her studies. Besides missing out on the social aspect of an on-campus education, she realised that distance learning also meant that she had no access to campus recruitment drives. This meant that without any connections, Prachi's dream of reading and writing for a living was likely to just remain a dream. Besides, even if she somehow found her way into the media industry, she could not afford to do an unpaid internship, a common path into such work. Her family relied on her income both for everyday expenses and to pay back loans that they had taken out for bigger expenditures like house repairs.

At first glance, Prachi – confident, speaking fluent English, pursuing higher education and employment in new services – aligns with the popular depiction of aspirational youth capitalising on the opportunities afforded by 'new' India. But Prachi's reflections on the constraints in her life, which she referred to as 'tensions' – and which she astutely linked to the uneven distribution of the benefits of liberalisation and globalisation through her everyday experiences – troubled her simple typification as an aspirational young woman. Instead, they highlight how for youth in the country – marginalised by gender, class and caste – upward mobility is largely a mirage.

This chapter engages, through a granular analysis of young women's efforts to enter work, with the discrepancy between the popular imagination and lived realities of 'new middle-class' lives. In particular, it explores how while education has seemingly become much more accessible, symbolising modernisation and development, the way it is acquired and the benefits it accrues vary hugely. These young women's narratives disrupt the imagination of a 'new' India, where rags-to-riches mobility is possible through a happy marriage of youth aspirations and economic opportunities by showing that the uneven terrain of opportunities locks lower-middle-class youth within structures of constraints in their everyday lives. The illusion of everything being just within (and just out of) reach may serve as the propulsion towards a 'cruel optimism' (Berlant 2011), but this chapter importantly shows that young women themselves reflect on the cruelty of their optimism. They recognise the constraints of their circumstances and criticise systems that lock them out of the opportunities that are supposedly abundant in post-1990 India.

'Pronouncing' English

Meeting me outside of work one day, Prachi said, 'Sheela can't *pronounce English* very well so whenever someone comes who only talks in English, *she put me in front*.' Over the course of the mornings I spent sitting around in the café, I noticed Sheela retracting to make coffee while Prachi confidently handled the customer interactions. Sheela herself confirmed her trepidation about pursuing an English-medium undergraduate degree, 'Yeah, I'll fill in the form for next year. But I don't know, my English isn't very good, so I don't know how to do it.' Like other interlocutors, Sheela had studied at a Hindi-medium government school and thus was not confident in her English abilities. At the café, the coffee-drinking English-speaking crowd expected interactions in English, so Sheela learnt a few standard phrases – 'Good morning, sir/ma'am', 'What can I get for you?', 'Have in or take away?', and so on – that served the purpose; the customers were, after all, not there to have long conversations with her. But she was particularly worried about pursuing higher education in a language that she was not comfortable with: 'I don't know, my English isn't very good, so I don't know how to do it.' 'Can you not do it in Hindi medium?' I asked. Sheela explained, 'No, but I also don't like Hindi. And here all my work is in English. I don't know English *perfectly*. So I'll have to continue … [learning English].' Sheela, like the other young women, intended to struggle through it in the hope that she could build a better, perhaps a more secure, future for herself. There is indeed evidence that English-speaking, besides being essential for entry into service employment, also impacts the potential for earnings (Azam, Chin and Prakash 2013; Shariff and Sharma 2013).

Like Sheela and Prachi, all interlocutors had studied at government schools. A key distinction between government and private schools is the medium of instruction; while government schools are usually 'Hindi medium', private schools offer 'English-medium' education. Ultimately, the difference between Hindi-medium and English-medium education lies in the life chances that each affords and perpetuates. My class privilege was apparent not just in my ability to speak English but in the *way* that I could speak English – fluently and naturally. My English-language skills are a clear demonstration of class reproduction; I learnt English first from my family and then in the private English-medium convent school that my parents sent me to.[1] In contrast, these young women's families were not English speakers; they were the first generation learning to speak the language to gain entry into service work.

Responding to the discrepancy between the backgrounds of workers and new requirements of service work, many skill centres providing employability training through short-term specialised and general courses have bourgeoned in low-income neighbourhoods in Delhi (Nambiar 2013). While these skill centres are aimed at skilling youth to meet the demands of service employment, some of them specifically encourage, mobilise and train young women to enter work, propelled by concern with the low female labour force participation rate in the country. In Dakshinpuri (and surrounding neighbourhoods), the most popular skill courses included basic computers, English speaking (Figure 2.1), administrative and finance software and retail management. As spaces that the interlocutors frequently mentioned and that seemed important to their entry into work, skill centres were important for understanding emerging worker subjectivities. The first time I visited Yuva Mandal, a skill centre in Begumpur, I went up a cemented staircase and was immediately greeted with 'success stories' posters on the walls of the open hallway (Figure 2.2). Most of the images were of women who had, with the centre's help, found employment at Burger King, Pizza Hut and PVR Cinemas. The manager, Mahesh, introduced me to some of the students at the centre and told me that they assess all candidates through the 'CAN' framework: commitment, ability and neediness (with the latter in particular referring to the low-income backgrounds of students being trained to enter semi-skilled service work). Yuva Mandal, he told me, charged a nominal fee for both specialised and general employability courses. The general course

Figure 2.1 An institute for coaching English in a residential neighbourhood
Source: Photograph by the author.

aimed to train students in information technology, spoken English and 'personality development', which I discuss further in Chapter 4. Following the completion of training, the centre attempted to place students with employers; it seemed to me that they served as a substitute for on-campus placements that young people in regular education had access to. The manager's office had a bookshelf to one side, and I chanced upon the titles *Get That Dream Job* and *Superfast English*.

Although Prachi had herself not enrolled in any skill courses, her younger sister, Priya, had been pursuing a general employability course, similar to the one Mahesh at Yuva Mandal had told me about. It was through this centre that Prachi came to know about job openings at the café. In recounting their experiences of entering work, many interlocutors explained that similar to a lack of guidance about education, they had had very little advice for their careers. They figured out job avenues for themselves either through neighbourhood or word-of-mouth networks – for example, a friend's brother may share a job opening at the company he is employed at – or through skill centres, both

Figure 2.2 A poster about 'success' at a skill training centre
Source: Photograph by the author.

directly and, as in the case of Prachi, indirectly. She was confident about her
English skills and thus her ability to secure this job. Similarly, Chandni said,
'I've never really failed at interviews. Yes, I've failed in two, in one they asked
for *proper British English*, that's not *possible* for me.'

But not all the women were as confident as Prachi and Chandni and were
only learning interview strategies through experience. I met Jahanvi through
her younger sister, who was enrolled in literacy classes at an NGO that I had
been spending time at. The first time I spoke to Jahanvi in her home, she sat on
her bed, cross-legged, and half-jokingly told me about how much she enjoys
getting men's attention as the only woman in the café she worked at in the Select
Citywalk mall. She came across as confident and funny and seemed to enjoy
her work. But as I got to know her, she shared her less-than-straightforward
journey into work. In the early days of job hunting, Jahanvi told me,

> I prepared a *résumé* first, then I went to each shop in the mall one by
> one. In shops they asked me to talk about *myself* in English. When I

did, they said, 'This is *myself*, like you'd say it in school, try to say it better.' But I didn't know how to do it. Then she said, 'Sorry, we can't offer you a job in that case.' Nobody had ever told me how to do it in the interview, like you don't talk about your father and sisters, you have to talk about yourself. *Ma'am* said, 'Talk about yourself, what have you done, are you a graduate?' I said, 'I could but not much.' She asked me if I know English. I told her I do but not very well.

While young women shared their lack of confidence in English fluency and highlighted the class differences between Hindi-medium and English-medium education, they also elaborated that English-speaking skills were a way to shed rural, or *dehaati*, roots and could even be a social leveller. I had met Ranjini through another skill centre. Ranjini was one of the successful alumni of the centre, and the manager had passed on her number to me. When I contacted Ranjini, she suggested that we meet at Select Citywalk on Friday. She was going to go into work for a little bit to hand in her manager training form and could make time for me after. Ranjini and I had a long chat seated on a bench in the landscaped outdoors of the mall. She had been working as a fast-food worker for the last two years and had recently been promoted to trainee floor manager, or TFM. Unlike the majority of interlocutors who had grown up in Delhi, Ranjini had moved to the city at the age of 13 with her family. As such, she had strong connections with their family village in the neighbouring state of Uttar Pradesh. The move to the city, and particularly learning English, had been a transformative experience for her, which she articulated as the key difference between village people and city people:

> These days there's not much difference between *low* and *middle class*; everybody has money, everybody has phone. *Chhote log* [poor or modest people] use the same things as *bade log* [big or rich people]. And with education, even with *government* education, everybody can speak English…. Those who come from the village, they are different. They don't know how to speak English, their education is not so good…. These days there's nothing in life other than *job* and studying…. When I lived in the village, my nature, my style of talking was similar to villagers. Here it's changed, I talk differently. I learnt to use words in English. My style of talking changed. When I went to the village, I talked differently, they all said, 'Oh she's only been gone for four days

and she's changed.' I said it's not like that. *Mummy* said we went outside because we wanted to change our children's *nature* so they can do better in life. If we stay like villagers, what's the point of that?

The taunt that Ranjini received in the village for speaking differently, and more importantly, for speaking in English, is not dissimilar to the mocking Prachi faced from her friends from time to time. But Ranjini emphasised that her family's move to the city would be for nothing if they did not change, if they did not learn the ways of the city and if they did not talk differently from the villagers. Jahanvi too, with practice, had gained confidence in her English skills; she felt proud of her transformation into an educated professional: 'Sometimes when sir calls, I have to talk a bit in English. *Papa* sees this and thinks I'm talking about such big work stuff. He wants my younger sister to go too but she's scared.' This need to shed rural roots is highlighted in Eileen Otis' (2011) research with migrant workers in the hospitality industry in Beijing too and points to emerging patterns of labour arrangements and relations; rural-to-urban migration is key to propping up the service sector through the provision of cheap and malleable labour. In India, rural-to-urban migration is incentivised through the decline of agriculture and the promise of better opportunities in cities through the expansion of services. While the women workers in Otis' research do not engage with English speaking as a necessary skill for service employment, they try to dissociate themselves from rural-ness through make-up and body language (which I discuss in Chapter 5); Otis suggests that these attempts are always already a failure since women are conscious of their shortcomings. Similarly, while Prachi spoke English confidently, many women hesitated because they felt that they were always going to fail at it.

In real everyday life, the interlocutors shared, there were increasingly situations where the ability to speak English could place you at a considerable advantage (and conversely that not being able to speak English well enough could place you at a considerable disadvantage). While Chandni had learnt enough English to ace job interviews, she was conscious that she needed to improve it to negotiate other everyday and future situations. Referring to her boyfriend, who came from a more secure middle-class background, she said,

He really wants both of us to study. When I went to his home, his mother didn't ask me if I can cook. She asked me how educated I am. Even if I want to study after marriage, I'm sure his father would pay for my education. His mother is a *housewife*, she hasn't studied much. When he got admission in *private school*, his father's *madam* pretended to be his *mummy*. My English isn't too good, so he keeps telling me to learn English. He says when our children go to school, he doesn't want to have to take a *madam* with him.

Once again using the figure of the 'madam', Chandni detailed a future in which, partly through her association with her boyfriend, who had already studied at a private school, and partly through her own efforts to speak better English, her children would be able to secure entry into private English-medium education. As part of the admission procedure, 'good' schools may interview parents to assess suitability. In a comical depiction of this situation, a popular Bollywood film, *Hindi Medium* (2017), showed the travails of a middle-class couple from Old Delhi with limited knowledge of English trying to gain entry for their daughter at a prestigious English-medium school in Vasant Vihar, a posh locality in Delhi. They move to the area and get coaching to 'refine' their manners, but their first attempt fails precisely on account of their inability to speak fluent English. Chandni's boyfriend's father was perhaps cleverer in his strategy of getting his 'madam', or boss, to pretend to be his wife or his son's mother at the admission interview. To avoid repeating this discomfiting situation in the future, Chandni wanted to learn better English.

Importantly, English-language skills are not just a resource to secure work in the service economy; they are an assertion of an identity, a status, a class. Prachi, since she could speak English fairly fluently, used her skills to establish dominance among her peers. She entered into several altercations with her colleagues during the 10 days of training she had to complete before joining work in the café:

> *Prachi: First of all, they tell us the history of coffee, how the coffee was brought to India, who brought it to India, and then how does it make, and what was the first reaction.* They told us goats had coffee plants and started dancing. They told us types of beans. All of this on the first day. Anyway, I'm used to it. I didn't have to memorise it, everyone else was; I understand and remember things. Then next day, you know what boys are like, someone asked does anybody have to still submit documents; I said I do. He said, what are you doing then, let's go. I was like *excuse me*. He was talking to me like I was his childhood

friend. *Is he really educated or not?* He used to talk in English, but it
was strange, like *I bhaunt that* (*laughs*). A lot of people wouldn't talk
in English, I do because I know I can. What do you think of my
pronunciation?

Me: Yeah, I think it's good….

Prachi: Yes, everybody said Prachi's English is really good. When I had
to fill in the form, I just said, *can you keep quiet, you're all educated
now, right or not?* Everybody shut up. Megha said these are boys,
it's good you just say it on their face. I said I don't care, if I don't like
something, I just say it. Then they all started calling me *ma'am*.

Prachi earned the title of *ma'am* through her fluent English speaking;
Chandni, by learning English, hoped to avoid the need for a 'madam' in
her future life with her partner; Jahanvi gained confidence and a place of
respect in her family by speaking English on the job; and Ranjini emphasised
English as the point of departure in the transition from rural-to-urban
lives or livelihoods. These multifarious interactions with the English
language demonstrate the complexities of young women's aspirations in the
globalising economy. They recognised the importance of English not only for
employment but also for social standing. They gained confidence and pleasure
from 'pronouncing' or speaking English. But, as their deliberations show,
their quest to speak English (fluently) derived from a sense of 'lack' – that
is, from the understanding that they had to compensate for not having learnt
English more naturally. As such, their claims to 'madam'-hood, to becoming
ma'am, were curtailed – while it was a temporary position they could occupy
at work, among peers or at a school in the future, they recognised that it could
easily be challenged.

Padhe-likhe log (educated people)

Education is fundamental for achieving full human potential,
developing an equitable and just society, and promoting national
development. Providing universal access to quality education is the key
to India's continued ascent, and leadership on the global stage in terms
of economic growth, social justice and equality, scientific advancement,
national integration, and cultural preservation … India will have the
highest population of young people in the world over the next decade,

and our ability to provide high-quality educational opportunities to them will determine the future of our country.

—'Introduction' to *National Education Policy 2020*
(Ministry of Human Resource Development 2020)

Chandni, who had attended the same school as Prachi, ended up working in the same café as her, although not for long; by the time I started frequenting the café in the mornings, Chandni had left after merely a few weeks of work on account of an argument with the manager. She was, naturally, hesitant to come to the café after the incident, but on Prachi's insistence, Chandni visited one day, ignored the manager while slightly keeping an eye on him and had a long chat with me. Prachi and Chandni had become friends at the Municipal Corporation of Delhi's (MCD) Sarvodaya Vidyalaya (*sarvodaya* translates to 'development or prosperity for all') in Dakshinpuri. Chandni said, although her heart was not entirely in it, she still persevered with finishing school because if she did not do well in education, her mother threatened to send her to wash dishes in *kothi*s (big houses), as domestic help in private households: 'I didn't want that to happen to me. So somehow I did my exams.' Although this threat may seem nebulous, it was very real for Chandni and her peers since they had seen their mothers doing paid domestic work. Indeed, Sheela's mother still worked as a domestic worker in a few households. These young women, working in cafés and other such new services, linked domestic work with poverty, relations of servitude and, most importantly, a lack of education. In India, paid domestic work, classified as 'self-employment', is overwhelmingly done by women, without any contracts, worker protection or social security. Far from declining, domestic work is an expanding area of work in India (Ray and Qayum 2009; Sen and Sengupta 2016). The young women in Delhi, then, firmly placed their belief in education as a strategy for avoiding falling into domestic work that their mothers had done or continued to do out of necessity.

The significant role of education as an instrument of nation-building is obvious – over the years, reports on the status of and plans for education published by the Indian government have emphasised the importance of educating the youth. Educated youth are the future of the country, and from the viewpoint of the youth, education is an instrument for better futures. Education, as a futuring practice, has, however, not necessarily delivered. While the reach of education has increased overall in the last three decades, educated youth have been unable to find work commensurate with their qualifications. Craig Jeffrey's long-term ethnographic research with young men in north India demonstrates this: in Meerut, Uttar Pradesh, he shows, young men enrol in never-ending college degrees as 'timepass' (Jeffrey 2010) while waiting to enter the next stage of their lives. In Bijnor, Uttar Pradesh, while young Dalit men have degrees, these are 'degrees without freedom' (Jeffrey et al. 2004) since formal education is unable to get them out of the loop of caste and class reproduction. These experiences find resonance in other parts of the world where young people, the intended beneficiaries of structural adjustment programmes, are waiting for the delivery of the said benefits (Auyero 2012; Mains 2007). There is, in contrast to this rich literature on young men's educational aspirations, relatively little research on young women's engagement with educational and subsequent economic opportunities. The gender gap in primary education has closed and even tilted in favour of girls, and it is rapidly narrowing in higher education (Ministry of Human Resource Development 2016).

For the young women in Delhi, education produces *padhe-likhe log*, or educated people, synonymous with high-class or *hi-fi* people. It was a potential route out of their working-class backgrounds, a point of departure from their parents' necessity-driven occupations. But these young women's investment in education was not limited to generational distancing; it extended to and intersected with the desire to free themselves of the gendered compulsion to domesticity (which I discuss further in Chapter 3). This might in some part explain why women pursued education with the utmost seriousness while their brothers were more likely to drop out of school and fall into 'bad company'. Prachi told me:

> [My] younger brother started hanging out with friends and neglecting his studies. So then that *tension* started about what he would do. Even now, we are worried about him. He goes away for whole nights, with boys you don't know, and he's even quit studying now. I feel sad about it.

The 'tension' (explored further in the next section) about her brother's behaviour is related to the tendency among young men not in education and employment (to use a policy category, these young men would be classified as 'NEET', which is an acronym for 'not in education, employment or training') to participate in 'trouble' in public places. Similarly, Sheela expressed worries about her younger brothers:

Well, boys in Dakshinpuri, all show off *style* in other stuff. They're all like that. They're more into play than work. Some are sharp at studies but still get into play. Like TV, phone … my younger brother, they are so crazy about phones. When I take my phone, they just get on to the net…. They play games, like *Action Mania*. They download games, that's what they do.

During one of my hanging-out sessions with Sheela, Prachi and Chandni at Chandni's house, I witnessed Chandni's brother and his friend, armed with a screwdriver and a set of pliers, setting up a television and a cable connection in their house. Chandni, echoing Sheela, said her brother was swift at learning things and was very interested in taking things, such as phones, apart and putting them back together. While young women commonly pointed to the innovative abilities of their brothers – being able to fix things around the house, teach themselves how to use computers or learn to drive quickly – they never espoused such qualities in themselves, instead relying on hard work and perseverance in obtaining an education to secure their futures. It should be noted that this does not suggest that families were more inclined to invest in girls' education, but rather that lower-middle-class men are perhaps able to access alternative models of aspiration that favour individual entrepreneurialism over education, regular employment and hard work.

The education that was accessible to these young women needs closer examination since it opens a window into the inequalities in the distribution of educational resources despite the national rhetoric of provision of high-quality education for all. Although, in recent years, there have been improvements in the quality of educational provision at government schools in Delhi, the young women had limited and poor resources when they had gone through primary schooling. The generally poor quality of public education has created a supplementary system of private tuitions as well as low-fee private schools (Arnold 2018; Banerji 2000; Kingdon 2020). In the lanes of Dakshinpuri, those who have completed education to class 10 or 12 commonly offer tuitions to earn a small side income. While these are usually 'affordable' for local residents, they are taken up at the cost of other expenses. Prachi told me, 'We couldn't afford *private school*, and I never asked my mother for *tuitions*. We couldn't afford that either.' Such decisions in low-income families are also often determined by gender. Rukmini Banerji (2000: 798) writes that in Ambedkar Nagar, a resettlement colony in Dakshinpuri,

… households follow complicated strategies to optimise schooling given the limited options available. One common strategy is to send the sons to a private school and the daughters to the local municipal school. Another strategy used by a number of families is to send the child to the municipal school but invest in tuitions at home, especially if the child is bright.

Inequalities of access to resources in schooling percolated into higher education too. An important feature of the higher education these young women pursued was that it was 'open' rather than 'regular'. 'Regular' refers to full-time enrolment in degree programmes, entailing the practices of attending daily classes, participating in co- and extra-curricular activities and socialising with peers on university campus. 'Open', on the other hand, refers to distance learning, whereby students go to the campus only once a week to attend classes and do not have opportunity for everyday interactions in spaces of education. All of the interlocutors had been pursuing undergraduate and, in some cases, postgraduate degrees through open or distance learning offered by Delhi University's SOL and the Indira Gandhi National Open University (IGNOU). They used the terms 'open' and 'regular' as markers of inequality of opportunities.

One Sunday, I accompanied Prachi and her friend Deepti on the yellow line of the Delhi Metro, from Saket to Vishwavidyalaya, on their trip to pick up their coursework from Delhi University. When we reached there, we were faced with shut grilled windows of the offices that distribute coursework for open-learning students. Prachi and Deepti were slightly disappointed, but we nevertheless enjoyed walking around the campus, and they took me to a streetside stall that they knew had a good reputation for its *chole bhature* (a popular Indian street food consisting of chickpea curry and fried bread). This was my first visit to Delhi University, and even during that brief time, the student in me picked up the excitement of being on a campus. Sheela, unlike her peers, was not enrolled in a degree programme when I first met her at the café. She told me she was short on money because '*Mummy* went to the village and there were those expenses.' Like Anamika, Prachi's elder sister, Sheela had also started working to provide for her family and to ensure her siblings' continued education. She was finally able to return to education in 2018, after her younger sister started working, thus contributing an additional income. She sent me photos of herself with friends at different spots on the campus. She told me she had been enjoying living the student life once again but soon returned to full-time work.

In that sense, it was obvious that for these young women, open education was preferable because it allowed them to work full time, and, thus, some had not even considered applying for entry into regular education. But it was also a compulsion in a number of ways, and when I probed further, more complex explanations emerged. Some noted that they had very little guidance from their schools and families about higher education. Pranjali, who was working as a financial assistant at an architecture firm and pursuing a distance education degree in commerce, had not made an active choice as such about her subject of study. When I asked her how she decided to pursue a degree in commerce, she said,

> Commerce? What do I tell you? I had no idea that there is Arts, Commerce, all of that. When I cleared class 10, I was very confused, my mind was *blank*. People kept asking which stream are you going into. Papa said Science, Mummy said whatever you like, somebody said Arts, somebody said Commerce. But I didn't know what these things were! People would suggest taking one or the other, but nobody told me what they are all about.

Pranjali's confusion about education choices reflects these young women's lack of access to social, cultural and, indeed, educational capital. For middle- and upper-class youth, educational guidance is forthcoming from families, schools and supplementary institutions of counselling and coaching; thus, they are not compelled to make their education decisions in a haphazard way. Some young women said they had never even considered regular college as an option since they did not know anyone in their neighbourhood who had gone to one. Prachi told me that although she wanted to go to a 'regular' college, there was a sense that it was not meant for them:

> From childhood, I wanted to study regular but everyone else thought where will they get nice clothes from to wear every day. I didn't think about all of that. I just wanted to study properly; I tried hard, but it didn't happen. I got really *depressed* at that time.

Prachi highlighted colleges or university campuses as securely middle- or upper-class spaces where regular education also requires participation in the college youth culture of fashion, consumption and leisure. For Prachi and her friends, not being able to afford 'nice clothes to wear everyday' meant that even if they made it to campuses, they would not feel like they belong.

This 'choice' of open, rather than regular, education had implications that Prachi and her friends recognised. They were placed on an unequal footing as compared to the middle- or upper-class youth who have access to on-campus education since it offers peer learning, learning support resources, networking opportunities and exposure to related activities that ultimately provide an advantage in the job market. In contrast, open education is conducted through weekly classes on Sundays that the interlocutors were often unable to attend due to either overtime work or exhaustion from work. They took exams at the end of the year after either opting for private tuitions or studying on their own with the help of textbooks and 'notes' from students from previous years. Mulling over her inability to get into a regular degree programme, Prachi said,

> I told you, no, I didn't manage to get in. I really wanted to. I went to Gargi College so many times. I didn't even know about all the different colleges. I got really disappointed. I was properly *depressed*. And then there was the issue of money, we need Rs. 6,000–7,000, where would we get that from. *Regular* costs a lot of money. I just wanted a chance, but it didn't work out. Only those with above 84 per cent got in. My father had an *SC certificate*, I didn't[2] … I used to get up in the morning, look through all the colleges, but I didn't get in anywhere. I then thought I won't study. Everybody said go into *open*, but I wanted that *mental stability* of studying everyday. Once I lose my focus on studies, I can't regain it. I thought I'd retry the following year, but then everybody kept telling me to not waste a year. Then Deepti was also joining SOL. I was very depressed; I just kept crying; mummy got really worried about me. Then I thought, fine, I'll join SOL, and then see next year. I started studying and sat for exams. I didn't get good marks, but I knew that already, *how can you expect someone to learn everything of a week in one day*. There's a crowd in the class, it doesn't work out. And then the results came out so late, I missed the second-year admissions deadline. But I didn't stop hoping … at some point, I tried to get stability on my own to study. Even now I can't afford *tuition*; I've always just tried on my own. Now I'm in my final year.

She insisted,

> If I do *postgraduation*, I want to do it *regular*. Then I can find something
> from it, I can get a campus, I could get an *internship*. But then I *blank*
> out, I don't know how to start, there's nobody around who can guide or
> help me. So I don't know how to apply, how to start….

Eventually, when Prachi got to the stage of applying for a postgraduate
degree, her apprehension, expressed similarly to Pranjali's as a 'blanking
out', about navigating entry into regular education fully materialised through
her circumstances. Working in a full-time job and making a significant
contribution to her family's sustenance, Prachi went for open learning again,
even as she recognised the failures of her second-tier education.

'Tensions'

Once we had determined common ground and started venturing beyond
the café, Prachi introduced me to her sisters – Anamika and Priya – who
were as different from Prachi as they could be. Where Prachi was confident
and assertive, Anamika was shy and a little nervous; where Prachi shunned
'frivolous' femininity and Indian sensibilities, Priya rejoiced in make-up,
heels and traditional clothes. This was, in part, Prachi suggested, a reflection
of their life circumstances. When Prachi's family first moved to Delhi, their
financial situation was comfortable; she told me her elder sister, Anamika,
had even gone to a private English-medium school. A few years later, her
father lost his job, and the family had to deal with adverse circumstances,
which meant that Anamika had to drop out of education and subsequently
find employment to support her mother in the maintenance of the
household. Anamika's efforts meant that her younger siblings could continue
studying. Prachi went to a government Hindi-medium school, but with her
entrepreneurial spirit, she taught herself English reading and secured work
in the café, providing an additional income to the family and easing their
financial circumstances. Since Priya, as the younger sibling, did not have to
struggle through circumstances as challenging as those Anamika and Prachi
had had to negotiate, she could, Prachi said, afford to be lighter in spirit and
being.

Although Prachi readily shared her life-world with me, she never invited me to her house. Instead, we hung out at either Chandni's house, in the mall or at one of the many food stalls close to the main road in Dakshinpuri. Over several visits and conversations with the interlocutors, I became more aware of the varied topography of Dakshinpuri. Chandni lived in a one-bedroom flat with her family – it was small, and we usually huddled together on the single bed in the bedroom. It was located just off the main road, making access to transport easier, and the street in itself was paved. Prachi told me her family had a small house that was in need of repairs; it was located in Ambedkar Nagar, a resettlement colony in Dakshinpuri. The term 'resettlement colony' refers to areas where people who have been evicted, usually from slums or *jhuggi-jhopdi* (JJ) clusters, are resettled. There are 55 resettlement colonies in Delhi, housing an estimated 1.25 million people (Centre for Policy Research 2015). While these resettlement colonies have brick, rather than makeshift or thatched, houses, they have poor conditions of living – lack of space and light, limited sanitation facilities, water logging and flooding are common. Prachi blamed their circumstances on her father and the breakdown of the domestic contract between her parents. Although they started out as a 'happy family' – '… the husband goes to work, the wife stays at home and looks after the children' – following her father's unemployment, which led her mother to become a domestic worker, '… my parents started fighting a lot with each other'. What especially disturbed Prachi was that

> … my father didn't try to secure our futures. It doesn't matter where we live, whether we belong to *lower class* or *upper class*, but all families think about how they want to bring up their children, but they didn't do anything. But our mother ensured that we go to school.

Having acquired an education, Prachi firmly placed her aspirations within the constraints that her family continued to negotiate:

> With *government school*, our fees were low, like Rs. 100–200 or less. Then life went on. I couldn't particularly focus because of the situation at home. What do I tell you about how I took exams; on one side my parents would be fighting, and I would sit there with my books open…. There would be crying and all…. So, we've mostly seen a life full of *tensions*. But even then, we haven't asked for much from life. Only that

if not luxury, we should get a peaceful life. All of us in the family have tried to contribute in some way. Tried to not go on the wrong track; I've tried not to add to the problems my mother and sister already have.

Prachi described the interrelated circumstances of her location and her family as 'tensions'. Other interlocutors also used the term 'tensions' to refer to the difficulties of their circumstances; they talked about the tensions they *had* – in that sense, tension seemed like something that an individual possessed but that, in turn, possessed, controlled and constrained individuals. Similar to Prachi, they had seen their mothers struggle to make ends meet when their fathers fell into long-term unemployment. They believed that if they were educated, they would not have to depend on their future husbands to sustain their livelihoods. Contrary to the understanding that 'heterosexual romance and marriage' is a route to escape their class position for working-class girls (Lawler 1999: 7), these young women saw marriage as a trap that could even result in downward mobility. Indeed, Prachi drew on her family's prevailing circumstances to clearly set out what she did *not* want for herself: '… with relationships and marriage, *I started getting angry on all these things.* These are root causes for problems in families … it's made a big impact on our lives.' Chapter 3 further discusses women's resistance to marriage.

While Prachi's family owned the house they lived in, Chandni, Sheela and other interlocutors lived in rented accommodations. Although this was a better quality of accommodation, the pressure to earn enough to pay rent each month was also a form of 'tension', as Ranjini shared:

> *Ranjini*: Private jobs don't pay so much, mummy papa always have *tension*. And we don't have our own house here, we're living on rent.
> *Me*: How much is the rent?
> *Ranjini*: Rs. 8,000–9,000. We have a whole flat. We can't just live like that, mummy papa also think we're all grown up.

Chandni's family moved flats because they could not secure an extension on the deadline to pay their rent, and Sheela's family moved because their landlord decided to increase the rent. These complexities are important to note since they betray the difficulties of categorising the 'tensions' young women faced in their everyday lives. This tension, Nandini Gooptu and Sneha Krishnan (2017: 404) suggest, is 'a heightened state of worry and anxiety felt by individuals' generated through the 'seemingly endemic and escalating stress and pressure of a society in transition and flux'. They also argue that '… "tension" is linked to a growing understanding of the self as an atomised individual suffering from a deficit of both social cohesion and ethical moorings'. While the interlocutors referred to their individual circumstances in describing their tensions, they nevertheless connected them to wider social and economic circumstances that restricted their mobility. Further, they attempted to rise above these tensions, but they were also acutely aware of the ways in which these constrained their lives – as such, their optimism was cruel, but their narratives were not devoid of reflection on this cruelty.

Prachi wanted to leave her café job for an internship with a media organisation, where she would be able to put her English skills, and particularly her interest in reading and writing, to use. By pursuing an undergraduate degree, she hoped that she might be able to somehow get a foot in the door: 'Anyway I'm still pursuing *graduation*. I think if I get *internship* in my area of interest, that would be good, that's what I want. That will help me figure out how to go about things.' But she also recognised that this was fanciful: 'But I have no contacts, and I'm not so outgoing that I can just go and find out. These days things happen through contacts only. I get depressed, but then I tell myself to relax. I feel bad; I still haven't been able to help my family.' Contrary to the suggestion that private jobs in the new economy are competitive and meritocratic (and hence open to all for fair play) as opposed to nepotistic government jobs of bygone days, Prachi pointed out that employment opportunities are still very much limited by who you know. In particular, employment opportunities where there is scope for progression, such as internships, are inaccessible without access to middle-class networks. For someone who had never received career counselling from family, peers or professionals, Prachi demonstrated an excellent understanding of the game. Relying on her entrepreneurial skills, she had figured out the route into media work: college education, followed by an introduction to a workplace through a contact, leading to an internship and, eventually, a full-time job. The knowledge of the game, however, rather than helping her on this path, made her aware of the difficulty and near impossibility of even setting out on this path – she particularly highlighted that her family did not have the social capital to enable her entry into this world; she did not have access to campus recruitment drives because she was pursuing distance learning, and, therefore, she simply did not know how to proceed.

This not knowing what to do, not having resources to draw upon, not being able to visualise a future was replicated in other interlocutors' narratives too. Pranjali, who had drifted into studying commerce, had some tentative ideas about her future, but they seemed to dissipate even as she talked about them:

> *Me*: What are your future plans?
>
> *Pranjali*: What I seriously want is to not live a life of *discipline*, 10–6 job every day, not the same life…. I want to do different things, I like variety. There's this *course, event management*, I read about it. There are *wedding planners, event managers, party planning* … all this, I'm interested in this. I want different things … like *projects*, that you finish, how did it go … this is what I like, I don't know when this interest will be fulfilled…. Then sometimes I think about staying and progressing in my current field, I keep changing my mind…. I think if this is my background, I should stay in touch with that…. Maybe I should just go into this…. In *event management* you don't know. In this your salary is fixed…. I don't have any other options anyway. Even if I want to leave, I can't.
>
> *Me*: So you want to leave?
>
> *Pranjali*: No, I don't want to leave. I just want to do something better. You can't grow in just one *company*. It's a small firm.

Similar to Prachi, Pranjali also had a clear vision of what she would like for herself in the future, but even as she described the vision to me, she retracted it with the recognition that options for her were not aplenty and that she would most likely have to stay and attempt to progress in the job she had at the time as financial assistant in a small architectural firm. Jahanvi, who had been working in a small café at the mall, also expressed an interest in trying her hand at different kinds of careers: she was pursuing an undergraduate degree at the time and thought she could put it to use by teaching younger students; she wanted to do this in the evenings alongside her 'day job' at the café. While we sat on the bed in her house, sipping tea, her neighbour – Soniya – dropped by. Soniya had worked at a fast-food outlet but quit that job to pursue fashion designing; she looked dressed for the role in a silver sequinned top, jeans and red lipstick. Jahanvi suggested that I talk to her to understand what girls want from work, slightly rolling her eyes and smiling. Soniya might have noticed Jahanvi's mocking tone, and the two of them ended up having an argument about what investment in work should look like:

Soniya: With *jobs*, the situation is that you have to wake up in the morning, deal with chaos, work, then come back and deal with chaos at home. For girls, it gets really *boring*....

Jahanvi: See, this is the thing; if I have to work, I just do. These girls are all like, oh, we have to wake up in the morning....

Soniya: No, it gets *boring*. See, I'm still working. I go to the school and do tuitions for kids, etc. So I'm quite busy anyway. I wake up in the morning, get ready at 7 a.m., go to the school by 8.30 a.m. Then I deal with children until 1 p.m., come back home around 1.30 p.m., have lunch. Then run to the 2 p.m. class, come home to drop off my bag and run again to the next class.

Jahanvi: You know, with me, if I'm told to work from 5 a.m. to 5 p.m., and then a second shift from 7 p.m. to 12 p.m., I'd do it happily!

Soniya: Your job is new, that's why ... I've got fed up. I've been in the *working line* for very long. I've been working since class 10.

Jahanvi: If you're fed up already, what will you do for the rest of your life ... (*laughs*)

Soniya: This is why I'm doing this course ... basic computer and general knowledge, everybody has ... we go to jobs with that, so we go from one place to another. Like, if you leave this job six months later, do you know if you would stay in the same line? You'll just go to another job with computer skills. This divides our attention. If you do an *exact* course, or you're a merchandiser, or you've done HM [hospitality management] or another good course, then you know this is your field that you'll go into. Then you don't have *tension*. *That's why* I'm doing this *course*. I've got fed up otherwise.... If you leave this job, you can stay in that field.

Jahanvi: But my mind is different, it wants to do everything. I like reading the person's *psychology*, I do that too when I'm standing at *retail* ... I enjoy that. I'd be happy to teach children in the evenings. I want to do everything ... *Ma'am* is talking about starting an institute; she said come teach young children there ... I don't want to go into one *line*, I want to do everything ... I can do a lot of things ... girls have to do this anyway, she works outside and manages things at home too; if she can do two things, I can do four!

While Jahanvi emphasised the importance of hard work, even working double shifts, Soniya suggested that one had to be smarter if they wanted to make a good career for themself. In Chapter 6, I will discuss the ways in which young women differentiated between 'jobs' and 'careers' as well as the circumstances in which they quit their jobs, but this argument between Jahanvi and Soniya is helpful here in understanding the ways in which women tried to envisage 'better' lives for themselves by pursuing different routes. Prachi, Pranjali and Soniya all wanted to enter more 'new-age' and glamorous jobs – media, event management, fashion designing – that could potentially be drivers for upward mobility. Prachi and Pranjali both understood that these were somewhat distant dreams and that these jobs would not necessarily offer them security. Soniya was hoping that by doing a specialised course, she would be able to carve a niche and rid herself of 'tension', even as she did piecemeal primary teaching to secure an income. Jahanvi thought that Soniya was being foolhardy and instead emphasised that one had to keep an open mind and grab whatever opportunity comes their way. Priya, Prachi's younger sister, would concur with Jahanvi. She confirmed Prachi's account of their lives being full of 'tensions' and, in particular, of their parents having 'tension'. She felt her part in assuaging these tensions was to contribute by bringing an income even if she did not like or want the work she was getting:

> *Priya*: Yeah, actually, there are lots of problems at home, so we don't want to give them more *tension*, they're just about managing anyway. If we have expenses, we figure something out. When I met you last, I went with *didi* to mummy's old *madam*. There's a wedding in their house. They needed someone urgently, so mummy talked to her. I didn't want to but I thought I'll do it, it felt awkward but….
>
> *Me*: What did you do there?
>
> *Priya*: I had to help them … it was all of that, housework….

Despite pursuing higher education and skill training, Priya was compelled into work she did not like: while not exactly washing dishes in *kothi*s, which the young women wanted to avoid at all costs, she ended up temporarily doing domestic work to keep the family afloat. A close look at such circumstances casts a shadow over the figure of the aspirational young woman – educated, skilled, professional – in urban India, demonstrating that young women's trajectories into education and employment are far from straightforward, and that even when women seem to have gained entry into new India through their education and employment, uncertainty about their futures looms large.

Middling aspirations

The duality of 'madam' and 'ma'am' was ubiquitous in the women's narratives – as the discussion in this chapter shows, it emerged primarily in relation to the ability to speak English, but it was also contextualised in the constraints of their lives. 'Ma'am' emerged with reference to others: me, their female managers, female business owners, employers who hired their mothers as domestic workers. Sometimes women shared with a tinge of pride that they were called 'ma'am' at work by their colleagues or customers. 'Madam', on the other hand, was used to mock, gesturing towards the aspirations they shared – to become 'ma'am' – but with the recognition that these aspirations were most likely unrealistic. In part, more educated than their parents and conversant in English, the women could shed the injurious subjectivities of *dehaati* (rural) and *chhote log* (low-class people), moulding themselves into educated urban women employed in service work. This afforded them an opportunity to become 'ma'am'.

But concurrently, they were aware that their education – Hindi-medium schooling and open degrees – was no match for the English-medium schooling and regular degrees of the securely middle class. They were also aware that their English, although of professional fluency, would never be fluent enough to make them convincing 'ma'ams'. They were also aware that, as a result, their employment options were limited to low-paid service work. At the time, most of the women were working in cafés, malls and call centres. Since then, e-commerce has emerged as a new niche of employment for women, but the divide has remained – without being able to achieve the English fluency that can only be gained by learning the language from an early age, they are confined to lower-paid jobs in domestic start-ups, while those from English-medium schools are entering better-paid work in multinational corporations. Therefore, even as they venerated 'ma'am' and used it as a term of respect, the young women who participated in this research also held the desire to *be* one at a slight distance by using 'madam' as a mocking term.

The settings where these subjectivities emerged are crucial to understanding women's adoption of the strategy of mid-identification. In preparing to enter service employment – through education, skill training and training offered at workplaces – women distanced themselves from those seen to be outside this new world, those who are not educated and urbane. They also asserted themselves as professionals, distancing themselves particularly from domestic workers and more generally from domesticity. Their ability to converse – and even argue, as we see in Prachi's case – in English offered them moments of pleasure, where they were able to assert themselves as 'ma'am', or at least potential or in-the-making 'ma'am'. But once at work, these opportunities diminished, and they became nervous about their English not being good enough. They also quickly realised, and the next few chapters will show this in further detail, that the promise of upward mobility through service employment was only a mirage. Outside of work, then, while Prachi continued to want to speak in English, most women thought it an unnecessary, perhaps even foolish, burden that indicated larger aspirations beyond their reach. When we hung out together, Sheela wanted to relax, shedding the work persona that necessitated English speaking; thus, she mocked Prachi for trying to be a 'madam'. This tussle between Prachi and Sheela, as well as the varied reflections of young women on English speaking in relation to their past and current 'tensions', shows how women practice mid-identification as a strategy to contain their aspirations. Rather than indulging in cruel optimism, they content themselves with middling aspirations.

Notes

1. Analysis of a recent Lok Foundation and Oxford University sample survey shows that the ability to speak English is closely tied to the social variables of class, caste, gender, religion and location (Rukmini S. 2019). The findings that rich rather than poor, upper castes rather than Scheduled Castes or Scheduled Tribes, men rather than women, Hindus and Christians rather than Muslims, and urban rather than rural residents are more likely to speak English point towards the reproduction of inequalities in education and consequently employment.

2. The issue of belonging in educational spaces in India is also intimately connected with caste. In recent years, the case of Rohith Vemula has highlighted the disproportionate number of Dalit or low-caste students committing suicide in India's premier institutes. It has also been linked with polarised discussions on reservations in public education for low-caste candidates. Most of the interlocutors belonged to low- to middle-caste categories; but Prachi, who expressed keenness for pursuing regular education, told me, 'I belong to SC [Scheduled Caste] but our SC card didn't work', referring to her inability to benefit from reservations in Delhi University colleges.

References

Arnold, Benjamin Mark. 2018. 'Global Aspirations and Local Obligations: An Ethnographic Exploration of the Construction of Classed and Gendered Identities in Three Delhi Primary School Communities'. PhD thesis, University of Exeter.

Auyero, Javier. 2012. *Patients of the State: The Politics of Waiting in Argentina*. Durham, NC: Duke University Press.

Azam, Mehtabul, Aimee Chin and Nishith Prakash. 2013. 'The Returns to English-Language Skills in India'. *Economic Development and Cultural Change* 61(2): 335–67. DOI: 10.1086/668277.

Banerji, Rukmini. 2000. 'Poverty and Primary Schooling: Field Studies from Mumbai and Delhi'. *Economic and Political Weekly* 35(10): 795–802.

Berlant, Lauren. 2011. *Cruel Optimism*. Durham (NC) and London: Duke University Press.

Centre for Policy Research. 2015. *Categorisation of Settlement in Delhi*. New Delhi: Centre for Policy Research.

Gooptu, Nandini, and Sneha Krishnan. 2017. 'Tension'. *South Asia: Journal of South Asian Studies* 40(2): 404–06. DOI: 10.1080/00856401.2017.1296633.

Jeffrey, Craig. 2010. *Timepass: Youth, Class, and the Politics of Waiting in India*. Redwood City, CA: Stanford University Press.

Jeffrey, Craig, Roger Jeffery, and Patricia Jeffery. 2004. 'Degrees without Freedom: The Impact of Formal Education on Dalit Young Men in North India'. *Development and Change* 35(5): 963–86. DOI: 10.1111/j.1467-7660 .2004.00388.x.

Kingdon, Geeta G. 2020. 'The Private Schooling Phenomenon in India: A Review'. *Journal of Development Studies* 56(10): 1795–1817. DOI: 10.1080/ 00220388.2020.1715943.

Lawler, Stephanie. 1999. '"Getting Out and Getting Away": Women's Narratives of Class Mobility'. *Feminist Economics* 63: 3–24.

Mains, Daniel. 2007. 'Neoliberal Times: Progress, Boredom, and Shame among Young Men in Urban Ethiopia'. *American Ethnologist* 34(4): 659–73. DOI: 10.1525/ae.2007.34.4.659.

Ministry of Human Resource Development. 2016. *Education Statistics at a Glance*. New Delhi: Ministry of Human Resource Development, Government of India.

———. 2020. *National Education Policy 2020*. New Delhi: Ministry of Human Resource Development, Government of India.

Nambiar, Divya. 2013. 'Creating Enterprising Subjects through Skill Development: The Network State, Network Enterprises, and Youth Aspirations in India'. In *Enterprise Culture in Neoliberal India: Studies in Youth, Class, Work and Media*, edited by N. Gooptu, 57–72. Oxford: Routledge.

Otis, Eileen. 2011. *Markets and Bodies: Women, Service Work, and the Making of Inequality in China*. Redwood City, CA: Stanford University Press.

Ray, Raka, and Seemin Qayum. 2009. *Cultures of Servitude: Modernity, Domesticity, and Class in India*. Redwood City, CA: Stanford University Press.

Rukmini S. 2019. 'In India, Who Speaks in English, and Where?' *Mint*, 14 May. https://www.livemint.com/news/india/in-india-who-speaks-in-english-and-where-1557814101428.html. Accessed 16 August 2022.

Sen, Samita, and Nilanjana Sengupta. 2016. *Domestic Days: Women, Work, and Politics in Contemporary Kolkata*. New Delhi: Oxford University Press.

Shariff, Abusaleh, and Amit Sharma. 2013. 'Inter-Generational and Regional Differentials in Higher-Level Education in India'. USIPI Occasional Paper No. 4, US–India Policy Institute, Washington, DC, May 2013.

3

Fast-forward | Tata Nano

Fast-forward

Chandni had started working in a quest to earn her own money and contribute to her family at the age of 16, a few years earlier than her peers. Her first job was at a call centre, which her father initially opposed but was compelled to accept when Chandni did not relent. Following the call centre job, Chandni went on to do administrative work in a smaller but more upscale office. While she was eventually disappointed at her lack of progression there, she still talked about it as a transformative phase in her life. It was while working there that Chandni changed from a naive girl with oily plaits to a fashionable young woman who drew the attention of boys (Chapter 5 discusses these bodily transformations). It was in this office that she met her first boyfriend – Rohan. Although Chandni was initially reluctant about this romantic liaison, the relationship was encouraged by her boss and colleagues. Chandni and Rohan started going out on 'dates', often with friends and sometimes just the two of them. She had told her mother about him, claiming '… she is like a friend to me'.

Rohan's family, Chandni told me, was fairly wealthy. They lived in Madangir, a slightly higher-income neighbourhood than Chandni's, and owned multiple properties across various cities. While Chandni's family, at the time, did not have any private vehicles, Rohan's family had recently bought a car – a Tata Nano – which he was driving around. The Tata Nano, it needs to be noted, is not just another car. Launched in 2008, the Nano, with its modest price tag of INR 100,000, captured the aspirations of a growing middle-class population who had previously only had access to motorbikes. As the world's cheapest car, the Nano was dubbed 'the people's car', becoming an object that symbolised India's capacity to innovate and integrate with global lifestyles. For Chandni, the car was a novelty, and her relationship with Rohan a learning experience. To her surprise, her colleagues, who had initially encouraged the relationship, now seemed envious:

> He [Rohan] used to take me out in his car. He had a Nano. Office people got us to talk, then they said Chandni turned out to be very *fast-forward*. But I wasn't attracted by his car or *bike*. I know besides love, you have to think of finances, but that wasn't it.

Similar to 'madam', *fast-forward* is a specifically gendered tag. 'Fast-forward', in simple parlance, means to play a recording at a very high speed or to rapidly wind it forward. Mobility and speed are, as such, of essence in defining something or someone as 'fast-forward'. In Chandni's context, then, her colleagues' use of the term is a reference to the mobilities that Chandni seemed to be gaining quite quickly from her relationship with Rohan. With Rohan's family being wealthier, the relationship portended upward class mobility for Chandni. His car and motorbike also afforded her greater physical mobility around the city and enabled their participation in the urban culture of 'dating', which could include the possibility of sexual exploration. Agitated by the tag of 'fast-forward', Chandni asserted that, contrary to her colleagues' understanding, her relationship with Rohan was not motivated by the promise of mobility.

Indeed, Chandni identified her employment, not Rohan, as the source of mobility. After all, she had met Rohan through work. Following her stint at the office, Chandni secured work at the same café as Prachi and Sheela; she already knew Prachi through school and had heard about this job opportunity through her. While she worked there for only a short time, she quickly also became friends with Sheela. After quitting from the café, Chandni did several 'events' jobs: she worked for a telecoms company, handing out leaflets and telling customers about the latest phone models; she also worked for a car company, calling customers to invite them to promotional events. In the course of these job changes, her relationship with Rohan ended, but Chandni's quest for mobility continued. Chandni learnt about various modes of transport as she navigated the city and work landscape. With practice, she became adept at hailing and bargaining with autorickshaw *wallah*s, traversing the expanding Delhi Metro network (Figure 3.1), sharing space with co-passengers on Gramin Seva autos (shared minivans) and going pillion on motorbikes when the opportunity turned up.

Modes of transport are more than just ways to get around the city; they are inextricably tied to constructions of class, caste, gender, sexuality and modernity. The 'old' manual rickshaws are now hardly to be seen around Delhi. There is a growing number of privately owned cars and motorbikes on the roads, while cab services by Uber and Ola have proliferated too. The rainbow-coloured lines of the metro are snaking their way to the outer reaches of the city (Sadana 2010), promising safety to women (Figure 3.2). Yet

Figure 3.1 Ongoing Delhi Metro work, with the sign reading 'men at work'
Source: Photograph by the author.

many are priced out of this world-class service for the masses, who then rely on cheaper shared services provided by three-wheeler autorickshaws and the Gramin Seva minivans. Of course, people often use these modes of transport in conjunction with one another. Chandni and her friends learnt how to navigate the city in the course of their employment, and as they became more familiar with the metropolis, they started finding leisure in it too. A woman who claims mobility for work is acceptable, but when the boundaries between work and leisure are blurred, the same mobility becomes suspect. Chandni and her friends' navigation of the city, then, reflects their imbrication in the story of India's growth and modernisation in specifically gendered ways.

Figure 3.2 Sign at a Delhi Metro station indicating 'women-only' coach
Source: Photograph by the author.

After a string of ad hoc jobs in the 'events' industry, Chandni hit a period of unemployment and concurrently, it seemed, a period of not going out. Partly, this was out of choice – Chandni wanted to focus on her studies for some time. Partly, it was out of compulsion – while she had been struggling to find employment, her mother had secured herself the position of a live-in nanny, leaving Chandni in charge of the household. But staying at home was not in Chandni's character. Her appearance changed; pointing to her unmade bed, she told me, 'When I'm not going out, I lose all sense of time. I haven't got dressed and I haven't even made the bed.' She described her days at home as endlessly dragging on, an experience that many interlocutors expressed through the refrain of 'boredom', explaining it as motivation for seeking employment (Islam 2020). While Chandni's parents did not impose restrictions on her, for many other women, employment provided a valid reason for 'loitering' (Phadke, Khan and Ranade 2011) or occupying public space. Thus, despite experiencing work as exhausting and exploitative (further discussed in Chapter 6), women made use of employment to gain mobility and consequently access to friendships, romance and leisure. Importantly, they positioned these practices in opposition to 'boring' domesticity. But these pleasurable pursuits were at risk of being seen as (gender, class, caste) transgressions, as women *trying* to achieve too much too quickly. This chapter explores the dynamics of young women's access to urban cultures, focusing on their mid-identification with the tag 'fast-forward'.

Sitting at home

Chandni tends to make it a point not to do any chores at home. During the summer of 2021, when I visited Chandni along with Prachi and Sheela, Chandni's mother made *kadhi chawal* (curry and rice) for us. Since there was a delay in getting lunch ready, Chandni's mother put together some snacks – biscuits and *namkeen* (savoury snack) – as well as orange Tang for us to drink. While she was rushing around getting things ready, we sat on the single bed in the only bedroom in the flat, with the air cooler sending extremely humid air our way; Sheela prodded Chandni: 'Chal, kuch to kaam kar le!' (Come on, do some work!) Chandni was unaffected by Sheela's reprimands, and eventually Sheela, who was sitting on a chair by the bed, decided to get up and help Chandni's mother. While we were eating, Chandni's brother came in, slightly limping; he had twisted and injured his ankle recently. Chandni seemed curt with him, although not unusually so, but once he left, she told us that she had not been speaking to him. She was putting on a show of being civil with him because 'I'm not going to be rude to him in front of *ma'am*; it doesn't look good.'

It turned out that Chandni and her brother had had a fight over housework. Chandni had been told off by her mother for setting a bad example for her brother by not doing any housework; Chandni believed this criticism was gendered, that she was only being told off because *as a girl* she was expected to do housework, and that he was using his slight injury as an excuse to not do anything. Her mother did not completely dispute this understanding; explaining it specifically to me, she said, 'He's a boy; if he does housework, but she doesn't, his friends are of course going to make fun of him. They will say your sister doesn't work in the house, but you do.' Chandni rolled her eyes at this explanation, and for the rest of the visit, she continued to make no effort to help her mother with food preparation.

Chandni had sought out her first job without telling her family; she had covertly attended training sessions at the call centre, revealing her activities only after the job offer was completely confirmed. When I asked where she had got such zeal for work, Chandni promptly replied, 'I have a problem with housework.' This problem with housework manifested many months later when she found herself unemployed, confined to home and not feeling quite herself. For young women, employment seemed to, at least in part, emerge out of the desire to not be at home and, consequently, to disengage from housework. While enrolled at school, they had a regular routine that entailed leaving the house and socialising with peers and friends. As discussed in Chapter 2, in contrast to school education, pursuing higher education through distance learning, with classes held only once a week, meant that they lost this routine. Employment, then, provided an avenue to reclaim their mobility; this was commonly articulated through the refrain that they did not want to 'sit at home' and that sitting at home (*ghar par baithna*) was 'boring'.

To avoid the problem of housework, then, Chandni persevered with employment; her father eventually acquiesced, but she expressed concern about the impact this would have on her studies since she was still in school at that point. He gave her an ultimatum: if she did not pass her exams, he threatened, he would make her 'sit at home' (*ghar par baitha dunga*). This relationship between education and employment is interesting to explore: while employment concurrent with school education was seen as a distraction (by these women's families and by them too), it became a worthwhile pursuit once they transitioned to higher education. More importantly and interestingly, employment even became a natural consequence of education when these young women had finished school, sometimes to the extent that 'education' and 'employment' were used almost synonymously. Jahanvi, like Chandni, had pursued employment opportunities (but only after completing secondary education) behind her family's back. When she disclosed that she had found a job, her father got upset; Jahanvi's mother was, however, supportive and presented a persuasive argument to her father: 'Mummy said to papa, what if there is a marriage proposal in which the family wants a *padhi-likhi ladki* [an educated girl]; will you ask Jahanvi at *end time* to go earn money then? Then he said OK.' In discussing how Jahanvi could have favourable marriage prospects, her mother equated being educated, or *padhi-likhi*, with earning money through employment.

In consonance with this understanding, young women asserted that their education would be a waste if they did not pursue employment and instead became 'housewives'. Chandni and Chitra had been friends since school; they looked for jobs as a team; over the course of a year, they worked together in a call centre and then in several 'events' jobs. Since they worked together, they could commute together, reassuring their families that they would be safe. But then they hit a low point: they could not find employment, particularly 'stable' employment, as Chandni put it; whatever little work they found was poorly paid, and often, they had to chase employers for payments. Chitra eventually gave into the frustration of the situation and decided to withdraw from work altogether. Chandni, unemployed and feeling bored at home, did not take this well, falling out with Chitra. Chandni blamed Chitra's lack of employment aspiration on her blind love for her then boyfriend. She said Chitra was now just waiting to get married and caustically remarked, 'Once this love runs out, Chitra will just be another *housewife*.'

To avoid housework and becoming housewives, young women then pursued employment, even if they did not find it fulfilling. Aarti, who was enrolled in the same undergraduate distance learning programme as Prachi, had started working straight after school and, similarly to Chandni, had done short-term work at several places. When I met her, she was working in the stationery room of a large multinational telecoms company, managing stationery stock and orders. Rather than being employed by the company directly, her contract was with a smaller company to which stationery management had been outsourced. While she did not particularly like her job, she said,

> Once you get used to a job, you don't feel like leaving it. You can't just be at home, you don't enjoy it, you feel like going out.... Even on Sunday, I can't stay at home. It gets really *boring* if you stay at home; I was home for one or two months and got really *bore* [*sic*]. My *life* became *boring*.

On the Saturday I visited Aarti in her office, it was quiet; there were only a few people in the office, and she did not seem to have much work to do. Her manager was sitting at her desk, having a relaxed day at work; Aarti and I sat together in the next room, lined with shelves neatly stacked with notebooks, ballpoint pens and other stationery items. In describing the time spent at home as that of all-encompassing boredom ('My *life* became *boring*'), Aarti emphasised that there was 'nothing to do'. Similarly, Deepti, who worked in a café, did not have a cordial relationship with her manager, but she was reluctant to quit:

> I think I should quit; there's no respect, no value for my work, so what's the point. But then I can quit, it doesn't impact him [the manager] any way; he'll find more staff. But what will I do just sitting at home? If I have another job, I can still think of quitting....

The rhetorical question 'What will I do just sitting at home?' came up often; interlocutors described their experience of being at home, even if only for short periods, as an endless stretch of time, a loss of routine and even a sense of despondency. In that, young women's experiences of unemployment do not seem vastly different from those of young men's; both Craig Jeffrey (2010b) and Daniel Mains (2007) observe that unemployment leads to an overabundance of time and hence to temporal rupture, which may be described as 'boredom', 'killing time', 'timepass', and so on. But, strikingly, although young women repeated that they had 'nothing to do' at home, their own accounts and my observations suggested that they actually had a fair amount to do when they were at home; at home, women were compelled into housework.

When Prachi was unemployed for several months, our WhatsApp communication was surprisingly brief: in part, Prachi said she had nothing to report and that all her days were similar; but when I spoke to her, she told me that she was frustrated and getting into arguments with her sister and mother about the distribution of housework among them. Indeed, it was not so much overabundance of time, but the pressure of housework on their time that young women seemed to resent when they were at home. In another way, their sense of 'nothing to do' can be understood as nothing to do that would be of value – this understanding reproduces the wider social invisibilisation of housework, but it also opens a window into young women's subjectivation, whereby housework renders them as non-workers and employment offers an alternative. Aarti explained that she had been able to excuse herself from housework through employment:

> See, I don't do any housework. My *mummy* doesn't even ask me. Sometimes she asks me, then says no, don't do it, you'll spoil it. She calls me, then she says no herself. So I just don't do it. When she says, Aarti, come, let's work, I say there's no point, you won't let me actually do it … I just use my phone, watch TV; if someone comes, I go out, do a little bit of housework. I wash dishes only one day a week, Sunday. I don't feel like it; I get so tired. I just want to sleep.

It took Aarti an hour and a half to commute from her home in South Delhi to her office in Gurgaon in shared cabs. She left at 7.30 a.m., returning around 9 p.m., just in time to get changed and pretend that she had been home for hours before her father returned from work. Deepti relied on a similar justification as Aarti's to refuse participation in housework:

> I don't do anything at home. I leave at 7 a.m., come back at 7.30–8 p.m. When I come back, I have tea; I can't be expected to do more work then. I tell *mummy*, how can I do it, will you leave all this work for me…. *Mummy* says you've become a boy, you go out of the house, you've failed even your brother and father.

With shifts lasting over 12 hours, it was natural that Aarti and Deepti were exhausted. Rosemary Deem (1986) suggests that rest is afforded to women who are valued as earning members of the family, whereas the drudgery and exhaustion of housework do not merit a similar getaway. But these transactions between employment, unemployment and housework were not straightforward. Division of labour is not just the distribution of work but also a construction of social hierarchies through a relatively rigid distribution of work, as these young women's accounts show. In particular, Deepti's mother's comment that she had *become a boy* refers to her unruly and wayward gender performance. As such, by refusing or at least expressing reluctance to do housework, young women were not simply withdrawing from and creating a small crisis of housework; they were also challenging existing gender and class relations.

Like other interlocutors, Sheela was not entirely content with the work she was doing, but also like other interlocutors, she was not ready to quit:

> I'll continue here because I'm unable to get out of it. If I leave this, I'll have to sit at home. If I change jobs, I want an *office job*, where I can work on a *computer*. More importantly, I want to continue working. This is why I don't want to leave this job … it feels good.

Sheela's mother left around the same time as her in the morning to work as a domestic worker in several houses and usually came back before she returned. With both Sheela and her mother working outside the home, I became curious about who does the housework. Sheela laughed and told me, '*Mummy* wakes up early to do it. I don't do it (*laughs*). *Mummy* keeps telling me to; she says ever since I started this *job*, I've become like a queen. I don't like doing work at home.' She extended her dislike of housework to staying at home: 'I can't sit at home, even on my days off, I go to Madangir [market] with my friend.' As we engaged in this conversation about housework, the café housekeeper, a man Sheela found rude, interrupted to say, '*Madam*, you will have to do it after you get married anyway.' He pointed out to Sheela that she was not from a *bada ghar*, or rich family, to be able to afford servants, and the man she would get married to might not even want her to work. Sheela became visibly annoyed with his interjection and retorted that she stayed away from people with this sort of thinking: 'I don't even talk to people who think like this.' The housekeeper advised her to give up her *badi soch*, or 'high thinking'; Sheela glared at him and then simply told me, 'He's spoiled my *mood*.'

There are several layers of power relations to unpack in this altercation between Sheela and the housekeeper. The main role of the housekeeper in the café is to clean; the (paid and unpaid) work of cleaning is globally predominantly done by women, but in India cleaning is also very strongly associated with low-caste people; further, it is stigmatised as unskilled and poorly paid work. The housekeeper's assertion that Sheela's life would be different after she got married might have been an attempt to put her in her place as a woman to be dominated by a man. But his further reprimand about Sheela's 'high thinking' might have been a reaction to the understanding that Sheela was transgressing her caste and class station by working as a barista in a café. Indeed, gender, class and caste are entirely inseparable in this scenario. While, unlike the housekeeper, Sheela's mother did not adopt an aggressive stance, her comment that Sheela had become like a 'queen' since she started working at the café was not dissimilar in its message. Deepti was rebuked for becoming a 'boy' and surpassing her brother and father (in their lack of contribution towards housework). It is interesting to note that both Sheela's and Deepti's mothers commented on how their attitude towards housework had changed after finding employment – that is, employment had caused a shift in the kind of labour they were willing to do. Further, their mothers' comments highlighted discomfort with, although not outright rejection of, young women's transgressions of class and gender.

When I started to think about the meanings of boredom in these young women's lives, I consulted Prachi (who by that time had also taken on the role of my research assistant) with some preliminary analysis. I told her that it seemed to me that many women were propelled into work because they felt bored at home; she confirmed that work provides a way to avoid housework, which women classify as 'boring', but she also noted that women may use boredom to displace necessity as the reason for work. In other words, by asserting boredom as the motivation for seeking and staying at work, young women distanced themselves from necessity. In part, this could be their way of distinguishing themselves from their mothers, who had done domestic work out of necessity; on the basis of their higher levels of education, they asserted their place in 'skilled' service work, rather than in 'unskilled' domestic work. But, in another part, Prachi said this narrative also served as an important signal to their managers. Working out of necessity implies acceptance of poor and unfair working conditions. She said employers mistreated them because the latter knew that they came from *chhote ghar*, or modest or lower-class families. By asserting that they were at work not because they *needed* to be but because they *wanted* to be, they indicated that they would not be submissive. Boredom, as such, is intricately located in the dynamics of not only work and home but more broadly emerging gender, class and caste relations in the context of work, home and leisure.

Going out

The world for these young women seemed to be divided into two: those who go to work and those who do not. While Chandni was openly disdainful towards Chitra for giving into being 'just a housewife', others expressed sympathy for their peers whose families did not 'allow' them to work. Aarti made sure that she was home before her father every day so that he remained unaware of her late return from work – 'If he knew, he would make me quit my job. It's different with *mummy*, different with *papa*' – but she considered herself lucky in comparison to a friend she used to work with:

> … I have a friend whose family doesn't allow her to go to a job. When I left the office, you know Navi's office, this girl left the office too. But now she's not happy at home, *obviously* nobody can be happy at home [*man nahin lagta hai*]. She wants to go into *fashion*, into *modelling*, but brother has said no. These kinds of restrictions can be there, like you can't go here, you can't go there.

For young women, one way to navigate the restrictions placed by families on their mobility – which, as Aarti highlighted and was abundantly evident through observations, were rife – was to find a job. Besides escaping the ennui of home (Aarti emphasised that it was *obvious* that nobody could be happy with staying at home), work also provided an escape from the surveillance of families for the bulk of the day; time spent at work, as such, was *their* time.[1] While for young men unemployment may generate a similar sense of restlessness, their overabundant time is usually expended in public spaces, such as at tea stalls, at corner shops and even on college campuses (Jeffrey 2010a). For young women, on the other hand, there were multiple demands on their time at home, rendering it 'collective' time (Davies 1989; Deem 1986). Work, then, was the only legitimate reason to traverse public space and claim time for themselves. And even then, they were not granted unquestioned access by their families; instead, they had to operate within restricted parameters of times and locations, only taking up work that was within a short distance from home and had daytime working hours. Prachi especially struggled with such family restrictions; over the years, she has had to turn down opportunities for better employment because they had been outside the radius that her family would accept. As Aarti stated, even though the *mahaul* – the social environment or the social fabric that these young women were embedded in – was changing, it still had some way to go. Their negotiations over mobility – their ability to get out of the house, occupy public space and participate in leisure – were contributing to creating flux in this social fabric.

Women's mobility enables their access to urban cultures of leisure, which include the interrelated cultures of romance, friendships and consumption. For many interlocutors, going to work was their first real foray into the city. Most of them had studied in government schools in or close to their neighbourhoods; their daily commute was, then, restricted to a small radius and on foot, often with friends. As school students, they had not had much independent access to consumption as a form of leisure. The markets they had frequented were also local markets. Even though they found work in cafés, shopping malls and offices that were not too far from their homes, they were located in areas that were removed, by distance and class, from their homes. Going to work, then, involved a commute through the city. Sheela, Prachi and Chandni told me that they became familiar with transport networks – buses, shared vans, the metro – once they started going to work and still, on occasion, felt nervous using them. Meeta similarly reported,

> At home, actually, you just can't pass time. Now when I go home, my sisters say you do get tired, but we feel bad staying at home. At least you go outside. You get to see what it's like out there; you've learnt how to travel.

Meeta's sisters' sympathy for her exhaustion and envy for her everyday adventures reflect how young women themselves felt about being at work. Importantly, work offered a window into the 'outside' world, beyond the insular space of home and neighbourhood that they had been in previously. But this was not straightforward or without its problems. Their access to transport was patchy, with bus stops and metro stations beyond walking distance from their homes. Buses were generally seen as overcrowded and hence unsafe; the metro was unaffordable. Most of them relied on Gramin Seva, a shared minivan service, to commute to work. Sheela said,

> I don't know about buses and I can't travel on buses … I've rarely taken buses, only ever *by chance*. If I come here early in the morning, I can get Gramin Seva. There's a lot of traffic here in the mornings, then *by chance*

I'd get a bus. It's so crowded, you can't really step on it. Also, on buses you have to look after your purse, etc. They get stolen.

Aarti, who had to make sure she was home before her father, relied on shared cabs to travel between her home in South Delhi and her work in the satellite city of Gurgaon. She did not have much flexibility with her office timings because, in her words, 'The biggest thing is even if I leave early, I wouldn't get a sharing cab. Travel is the problem here.' Everyday travel was clearly an issue because of a lack of reliable and affordable transport, but learning how to travel and putting it to other uses could also be an adventure.

Chandni and Rohan had informally hung out during office parties and informal gatherings before officially going out:

> … with Rohan, first time we met, with ma'am … I had gone with ma'am, sir, Sumna, Rahul *bhaiyya*, her boyfriend. Sumna had brought her car; she belongs to a good family. At that time, I was feeling quite *middle class* among all those *high class* people.

While Chandni initially felt out of place with her colleagues who owned cars, she soon moulded herself to fit into the environment, seeing it as an opportunity for personal development. This was particularly made possible by her going out with Rohan, who, from Chandni's description, seemed like an archetypal young man of new India (Philip 2022):

> I'm glad I didn't land up with an *awara*[2] [useless] boy from Dakshinpuri…. He's doing BCA [Bachelor of Computer Applications] at the moment; *he's very intelligent in computer*. He wants to *become a software developer*. He doesn't want to live here. He wants to go to either Singapore or Bangalore, because that's where software developers are. I didn't know all of this before; I learn quite a lot from him.

For Chandni, Rohan was the source of information about this new India, where more people are able to afford cars and dream about jobs in the growing IT sector. A few years later, Chandni bought a Scooty, a moped that has been marketed as the vehicle of the young urban woman's freedom (Krishnan 2020), but never learned to drive it, and eventually her brother started using it. In Dakshinpuri, the narrow streets were lined with plenty of motorcycles, all belonging to men, providing them a more convenient, if expensive, mode of transport. But a car was not to be seen in her neighbourhood. Her relationship with Rohan was a partial entry into the world where mobility was possible, but this relationship also earned her the tag of being 'fast-forward'. Tellingly, Chandni associated being friends with boys with the act of going to the office; it was almost a natural (and desirable, as far as she was concerned) consequence. Aarti too saw her work as an opportunity for romantic liaisons but also, more broadly, for engaging in cultures of romance. Beneath the surface of a relaxed Saturday, when I visited her in the office, there was actually quite a lot going on: when we went down to the food court for lunch, Aarti suggested that we go meet the office boys later on; she had told them about my visit, and they were curious. She warned me that they could be a little uncouth but that they meant well. Deep diving into office romances, she excitedly told me,

> You know the sir upstairs, that's my supervisor's *lover*.... This other sir, he's been transferred, he had a nice *way of talking*, like he would give equal importance to everyone. The rest of them don't know how to talk, you know, they're actually not even educated. They've done only 10 or 12; they don't know much, but they think they're so *smart*. You know, like Pandey, he boasts about so many girlfriends; even smart guys like Salman Khan[3] don't have that many girlfriends.

Her interest in this office gossip explained in part why she did not feel bored on a quiet day in the office, while life at home, on the other hand, was entirely boring. She spent a considerable amount of time talking to me about the men in the office, categorising them in terms of whether they knew how to talk to girls – in other words, whether they were urban and *cultured* enough to know how to *properly* and respectfully interact with women:

> There's one sir who would be very happy to meet you; he's very nice. I talk to him on the phone. Him and another sir, their *way of talking* is very nice. They can talk to girls. The rest of them are *taporis* [loafers]. Another sir is also very *soft spoken*.

Since Aarti categorised her peers as *taporis*, she argued with exasperation that although her mother suspected her of having a boyfriend at work, '… really, is there anyone in my office who I could like?!' She did have a boyfriend though, whom her mother was completely unaware of, in large part because her long hours at work allowed her an escape from her family's surveillance.

It was not just romance that young women sought and gained through work. Chandni had been friends with Prachi in school, but like other young women, once she had completed her school education, Chandni's avenues for meeting people, making new friends and participating in social activities became limited. It was therefore a no-brainer for Chandni to apply when Prachi told her that there was a vacancy in the café she was working in. Chandni and Sheela were initially co-workers and then became friends; over the years they have cultivated their friendship beyond work, and when I visit now, I almost always meet the two of them together. Chandni did not last long in the café; she did not like the manager and found the work to be a constraint on her life, but in the brief spell of time that she worked there, Prachi told me, 'Sheela, Chandni and I travelled together very nicely, very lovingly.' With their houses located within close vicinity, Sheela, Prachi and Chandni could arrange to travel together – sometimes Sheela and Chandni got annoyed with Prachi for being late in the mornings, but they could conveniently share the evening ride back home after work. Chandni had previously worked with Chitra in a call centre, relying on one another for company while travelling as well as for managing difficult work situations, including sexual harassment:

Call centres are bad that way, especially smaller ones…. Both Chitra and I went together; we used to protect each other; we used to protect Pooja [another colleague] too. She was very naive…. He [the boss] tried to be *extra friendly* with me once, so I said to him, *sir*, you know you're like my father…. He didn't touch me, but he tried to be *over friendly* … I didn't say much, but I said this much. Then Chitra came into the room. He then said, actually I'm a *bachelor*. I retorted, oh really, you look quite old. Well, at least you're like an elder brother; all my elder brothers are married. Chitra told him to not be *over friendly*. I couldn't be so straightforward. Chitra is very straightforward though. So when we found out about Pooja, we went to him, and said what is this about. He used to touch her thighs and such things. We told off Pooja too.

Clearly, for Chandni, Chitra had been a source of support at work, especially in the early days of entering the unfamiliar territory of call centres.

That might explain, in part, her severe disappointment when Chitra was no longer willing to look for work with her and was indeed not looking for work at all. For some women, the ability to travel to work with a friend was what enabled them to work in the first place. Jahanvi thought about work when her friend Neeraj suggested it. Jahanvi's father was opposed to her entering work; when she first started looking for work, she told her family that she was going to meet Neeraj. Jahanvi said, 'Papa knows how much Neeraj helped us and he trusts her.... That is why I value her so much and consider her my *best friend*.' It was under the pretext of spending time with a trusted and safe friend that Jahanvi was able to secure her first job in a doughnut café in the Select Citywalk mall. There, learning to assemble and serve doughnuts and coffee, Jahanvi met new people and made new friends for the first time since leaving school. When Jahanvi moved on from her first job to work in a café, also in the same mall, one of her co-workers, Sarita, followed. I was not aware of the association between them when I first met Sarita. I asked her how she had found this job, and she told me,

> *Sarita*: Through Jahanvi. I had asked her to tell me if there's a job. So she told me ... I knew Jahanvi from [the other café].
>
> *Me*: Okay ... what happened in the interview here?
>
> *Sarita*: Not much ... I didn't feel like doing it for Rs. 9,000 [per month], but *sir* said they'll increase it in two months ... I thought it's better to do this than sit at home. When we're here, we find out about jobs. You go somewhere, you meet someone, you find out stuff. It makes a difference as compared to sitting at home.

Sarita summarised how a lot of young women felt about going to work that they did not particularly like or want to do – being at work provided a space for networking that could open up opportunities later, and, importantly, that was a big gain over just sitting at home. When Sarita had been between jobs, she decided to, rather than sit at home, join a short-term course at a local skill training centre:

> ... when I wasn't working recently, I did a course there [at a skill training centre]. I didn't need to, but I was sitting at home, so I thought this can be *timepass*. I did three months training, but then I left and joined this job. So I didn't complete it. It was a *computer course* too, for *code* ... but they don't get many jobs.

Mahesh, the manager at Yuva Mandal, a skill training centre, found some of these patterns of women's employment frustrating. The first thing, he said, is that girls don't want to go far away to work. The other concern, which he tries to dissuade his students from, is finding a friend to go with; girls are reluctant to go to work on their own. He said, 'Often because of these issues, girls keep waiting for the right opportunity.' Mahesh encourages them to take up whatever is offered because he thinks it is important for them to build experience before they can choose where to work and with whom. Mahesh's advice really seemed converse to young women's mode of operation in the job market, perhaps because, while Mahesh identified lack of confidence as the issue, for young women, work and friendships were closely interwoven in various ways. Work and friendships were mutual – women found work through friends and friends through work. These friendships, then, not only served the function of companionship or sociability but also acted as resources for finding, going to and sustaining work (Andrew and Montague 1998; Green 1998).

Avoiding 'tensions'

Just as work was about seeking some things – mobility, freedom, romance, friendships, resources – it was also about avoiding other things: domesticity, surveillance, tensions and problems. While domesticity and surveillance were a direct converse of mobility and freedom, tensions and problems are a bit more difficult to categorise. As discussed in Chapter 2, 'tensions' referred to long-standing familial problems that the women had experienced and that were linked to the lack of employment, usually that of a father or a brother. I specifically say 'lack of employment' here, rather than unemployment, because many women articulated the need to pre-empt these concerns by seeking and joining work in the first place. Their tensions and problems ranged from domestic conflicts to gossiping and falling into bad company. Prachi had observed these in her family; her father had been unemployed for a long time, and she felt frustrated that he had seemingly made no effort to redress the situation. She noted that when her father lost his job, things started going downhill for her family:

> To this day, I still don't know what he's been doing. Ever since he left that job, there's no record of him of having properly worked somewhere

or of having brought a salary home. After that my parents started fighting a lot with each other. I don't know if it's true, but my mother started accusing him of having affairs. I don't know if it's true or not; maybe it's in her mind, but I didn't want to find out much; it's between husband and wife. Their fights have continued to this day, throughout our childhood, that's what I saw.

Besides the financial loss that pushed her mother and elder sister into work, her father's unemployment, Prachi said, led to discord between her parents, which had put her off the idea of romantic relationships and marriage:

> If I sit down to explain our family's *problems*, seriously … sometimes I really think about how I have managed to survive and study so much in my family. My parents never got along; they're always fighting. This is why I have a problem with getting married too (*laughs*).

While Sheela's and Chandni's stories are slightly different – Sheela did not recall a time when things were ever good for her family, and Chandni said that her parents were still living in harmony – both of them also narrated a similar trajectory of their fathers being in relatively good jobs, losing those jobs and never going back to work, causing various kinds of problems for the family. In part, the loss of income, particularly in cases where it was the sole income, meant that the family was exposed to the risk of falling out of their upwardly mobile trajectories and back into poverty. The breakdown of the male breadwinner norm alerted young women to the vulnerability of relying on marriage to achieve stable and established lives. It further strengthened their resolve to find and stay in employment. It also explains their rejection of domesticity; domesticity, they realised, did not secure livelihood and, more importantly, did not secure a *good* livelihood. Sheela described her motivation to find employment almost as a retaliation to her father's misbehaviour and abuse:

> I don't talk to *papa*; it's been a few years. I don't want to talk to a person who can't talk with respect, who swears and abuses. This is why I don't think about the family. I only think of those who care for me, who love me; why should I think of those who only wish bad upon me? So, I just let people say whatever they want to. I know what I'm doing is right, so I do it. I like working, wearing *jeans*, so I do it, and I go out of the house.

Work, in that sense, afforded young women a sense of independence, perhaps better described as freedom from dependence on men's goodwill to provide for them. Sheela emphasised the itch she felt if she stayed at home: 'Yes, I can't sit at home, even on my days off, I go to Madangir with my friends. I force them to go.' Participation in paid work was often articulated as a reclaiming of their time but also, more importantly, as a *worthwhile* use of their time. While Prachi considered romantic relationships a waste of time, Sheela was also strongly opposed to the neighbourhood culture of gossip:

> *Me*: … in your neighbourhood, other girls go to work? What jobs are they doing?
>
> *Sheela*: Yes, they do. They're mostly working in *offices*. I've talked to one of them; she does *data entry* work in Nehru Place. I see her from time to time … I don't get to talk to many of them. Actually I don't talk to people in my *gully* [lane]. I don't like talking there. I only talk to those who talk about good things. I don't like gossip, that's what girls do; they talk about boys, and I'm not interested.

These notions of what is a worthwhile use of time and, conversely, what is a waste of time were integral to their engagement with emerging subjectivity as professional women; they distanced themselves not only from domesticity and housewives but also from those who were not actively engaged in improving their lives through work. Mostly, this distancing or disidentification, an emphasis on who they *do not* want to be, was done through reference to other women. But they also pointed to male members of their families to express concern over unemployment. Their fathers' unemployment had been a major source of their families' tensions, but they also found the next generation of men – their brothers – quite concerning. Many of these women's brothers had dropped out of school and were either doing some ad hoc work or were unemployed and simply 'roaming around'. In most cases, families did not rely on young men's incomes since even when the men were working, they claimed their incomes, much like their time, for themselves. Chitra, who after much struggle gave up looking for work, upsetting Chandni in the process, told me that her father was disabled and unable to work; her brother, on the other hand, worked but '… he drinks and all…. That's the *problem*; you can't tell everyone … this is the *problem*; that's why I get annoyed with *job* people when they don't pay, they don't understand.'

Both Prachi and Sheela were also concerned about their brothers veering off course. Prachi's brother, much to her regret, was not even '10th pass' – that is, he had not completed school education. Without basic qualifications, his job options were limited. He had found work as a peon in an office, but it was low-paid contract work without any possibility of progression. Sheela also observed that young men are likely to fall into bad company and waste their lives. The women were critical of young men's indulgence in 'style' – mobile phones, jeans, hair gel – even though, as Chapter 5 will show, they too found pleasure in stylising themselves. The difference, they pointed out, was that women's style was in conjunction with the virtuous pursuit of education and employment, whereas men pursued style *instead of* education and employment. Further, part of men's style or attempts to 'look cool' involved other troublesome behaviours too, including hanging around on the streets, harassing women, partaking in shady small businesses or enterprises, drinking and doing drugs and gambling to make quick money. While women believed in education and employment as panacea for their 'tensions' and 'problems', masculine value was attached to the ability to somehow manipulate the system. Young men did not often succeed at making a living out of manipulating the system, but they seemed to take pride in their attempts nevertheless. On my visits to Dakshinpuri, I saw more men than women on the streets, but the significant difference was in their public behaviours: the women always seemed to be *on their way* to somewhere; men, on the other hand, were commonly just standing around in groups, chatting, laughing and sometimes eyeing and harassing women. Women, even when they indulged in 'timepass' in between jobs, participated in more 'productive' activities, such as doing a skill course at a nearby training centre.

Women emphasised that going to work, leaving the house, made them feel good. Chandni likened herself to her unmade bed when she was not employed: without a routine, she did not have the motivation to start her day with getting dressed; the day stretched endlessly. She identified similar behaviour in her mother too. Showing me her photos, she said, 'This is *mamma*, when she used to stay at home; she looked *aged*, but since she started working, no one can tell. She looks nicer than me.' Going to work, Chandni believed, had injected her mother with youthful energy and had a dramatic effect on her appearance. With strong investment in the idea of work, the young women still had to negotiate the terms and conditions of their employment with their families; as unmarried women, they realised that this might become even more difficult after marriage. They were hoping to be able to negotiate this by finding families who would be supportive of their employment. Neha, a 20-year-old sales assistant who was engaged to be married, told me that her fiancé's family was not just supportive but even encouraging of her employment:

> *Neha*: Yes. They said you get nothing from sitting at home. Unless you go
> outside and do something, you won't get anything. Because in the
> future that's to come, who knows what will happen with whom; no
> one knows. In the house, there's your mother-in-law, you're there,
> you say something, things unnecessarily get out of hand; there's no
> point to it.
> *Me*: That's what happens at home …
> *Neha*: Yes, that happens at home. Better than that, go out and do a job;
> *mummy* will also be *tension-free*, you will also be *tension-free*.

Neha was pleased to be marrying into a family that realised that spending too much time at home can lead to restlessness and unnecessary conflicts. In this case, the family saw the scope for a particularly gendered conflict between mother-in-law and daughter-in-law if both were to stay at home. As a woman of the new generation, Neha could help avoid familial discord or 'tension' by going out to work and letting her mother-in-law retain the domestic reins.

As such, for women who were out of employment, boredom did not lead to 'trouble', as has been noted in the case of unemployed men, including these young women's brothers. Instead, women linked it to poor mental health as well as conflicts within the family. They did so concurrently with complaining about exhaustion from long hours of commuting and working. Further, while workplaces were not free of hostilities, these did not weigh upon women in the same way, perhaps because their time at work was limited as opposed to the endless stretches of time at home. Thus, they posited employment as an avenue where they could choose friends, develop new relationships and, importantly, spend time in the 'outside' world.

Middling mobility

Employment offered women a chance to be 'fast-forward', to be mobile, and they took it gladly. By going to work, women had a valid reason to leave the space of home and their neighbourhoods. It enabled their access to leisure by making them familiar with ways to get around the city and consequently with urban cultures. They found friends and boyfriends through work, creating networks of support and resources, and went out for pizzas and dates. This participation in urban cultures also signalled, to a certain extent, class mobility. They could inhabit the spaces and partake in activities that they otherwise usually serviced as sales assistants, baristas, customer service assistants, and so on. But when the tag 'fast-forward' was used or implied by others, it took on a disdainful and suspect tone. Chandni's colleagues used the term for her mobility; however, it was not mobility that she claimed through her employment but rather mobility that had been enabled by her romantic relationship. She retorted by asserting the value of her employment and her relationship as only a by-product: she wanted to claim mobility, be fast-forward, but on her own terms, through her own efforts, rather than by relying on a romantic relationship.

In claiming fast-forwardness, women distanced themselves from the spaces and subjectivities associated with their homes and neighbourhoods. They did not want to be housewives and disdained (and sometimes sympathised with) their peers who went down that route. They also did not want to participate in the neighbourhood gossip circuit, seeing it as a waste of time. Their evaluations of time, whereby staying at home was 'boring', demonstrated a broader culture of prioritising economically productive activities over social reproduction and sociality in general. But these emerging temporalities were imbricated in their social fabric in other ways too. The women had witnessed that men and domestic or marital arrangements were not reliable sources of livelihood and could even lead to, as in the case of Prachi's, Chandni's and Sheela's families, downward mobility. By being fast-forward themselves, women made sure they were not stuck or trapped in the station assigned to them as lower-middle-class women.

Fast-forwardness or mobility, as such, carried multiple meanings that women engaged with variously at different sites. This chapter shows that these multiple meanings — physical mobility, independence, participation in leisure and urban cultures, class mobility — emerged in relation to young women's everyday activities, ranging from employment and education to housework and leisure. But most importantly, the implication changed dramatically between women's own claims to the reference and others' use of the reference for them. When alleged to be fast-forward, young women's desires — sexual, material, social — were challenged as transgressive of their gender, caste and class fabric. As with the dual meaning and use of 'madam' and 'ma'am', 'fast-forward' too muddied their assertions of independence through employment, compelling them to moderate it by shaping it through the virtuosity of employment. This boundary-making between propriety and impropriety is further discussed in the next two chapters.

Notes

1. This upends the generally accepted understanding that industrialisation led to a split between 'work time' and 'own time' (Thompson 1967). It is arguable that for women, in the interplay between market and social forces, this split has never been neat, clear or straightforward.
2. *Awara* roughly translates to 'loafer'. It is usually used as a pejorative term for men, particularly those who are unemployed and consequently roam around aimlessly, possibly harassing women. Chandni was pleased that her boyfriend did not qualify as *awara*; instead, he was from an educated family and had good employment prospects. His good qualities were reflected in his friend circle, who Chandni insisted were 'only good guys, those from *high society*, those who can understand … [their relationship]'.
3. Salman Khan is a popular Bollywood actor. He has enjoyed mass appeal with audiences, particularly men, for playing the 'bad boy' hero on screen (Shields 2017).

References

Andrew, Alison, and Jane Montague. 1998. 'Women's Friendship at Work'. *Women's Studies International Forum* 21(4): 355–61.

Davies, Karen. 1989. 'Women and Time: Weaving the Strands of Everyday Life'. PhD thesis. Lund University.

Deem, Rosemary. 1986. *All Work and No Play? The Sociology of Women and Leisure*. Milton Keynes: Open University Press.

Green, Eileen. 1998. '"Women Doing Friendship": An Analysis of Women's Leisure as a Site of Identity Construction, Empowerment and Resistance'. *Leisure Studies* 17(3): 171–85. DOI: 10.1080/026143698375114.

Islam, Asiya. 2020. '"It Gets Really Boring If You Stay at Home": Women, Work and Temporalities in Urban India'. *Sociology* 54(5): 867–82. DOI: 10.1177/0038038520934995.

Jeffrey, Craig. 2010a. *Timepass: Youth, Class, and the Politics of Waiting in India*. Redwood City, CA: Stanford University Press.

———. 2010b. 'Timepass: Youth, Class, and Time among Unemployed Young Men in India'. *American Ethnologist* 37(3): 465–81. DOI: 10.1111/j.1548-1425 .2010.01266.x.

Krishnan, Sneha. 2020. 'Scooty Girls Are Safe Girls: Risk, Respectability and Brand Assemblages in Urban India'. *Social and Cultural Geography* 23(3): 1–19. DOI: 10.1080/14649365.2020.1744705.

Mains, Daniel. 2007. 'Neoliberal Times: Progress, Boredom, and Shame among Young Men in Urban Ethiopia'. *American Ethnologist* 34(4): 659–73. DOI: 10.1525/ae.2007.34.4.659.

Phadke, Shilpa, Sameera Khan and Shilpa Ranade. 2011. *Why Loiter? Women and Risk on Mumbai Streets*. New Delhi: Penguin Books India.

Philip, Shannon. 2022. *Becoming Young Men in a New India: Masculinities, Gender Relations and Violence in the Postcolony*. New Delhi: Cambridge University Press.

Sadana, Rashmi. 2010. 'On the Delhi Metro: An Ethnographic View'. *Economic and Political Weekly* 45(46): 77–83.

Shields, Amber. 2017. 'Salman Khan: Counteracting Offscreen Transgressions with Onscreen Heroism'. *Celebrity Studies* 8(2): 355–58. DOI: 10.1080/ 19392397.2017.1311637.

Thompson, Edward P. 1967. 'Time, Work-Discipline, and Industrial Capitalism'. *Past and Present* 38(1): 56–97.

4

Middle class | Smartphones

Middle class

The day Sheela brought her new phone into work, she clutched her bag extra tight on the Gramin Seva, a shared minivan that she took for her daily commute (Figure 4.1). In the café, Sheela had tucked the phone into her trousers pocket. She took it out carefully and showed me, putting it on the café counter and pressing the home button so the screen would light up. Both of us admired the display – the colours were bright and the images sharply defined. She swiped it open and demonstrated the quality of the camera lens too – with inbuilt 'beauty' filters, I could tell and Sheela was convinced, this was going to be a great 'selfie' camera. She wiped the screen gently with a paper tissue to rub out the finger marks it had incurred in the course of showing it to me and slipped it right back into her pocket. This was by no means the first smartphone that Sheela had used, but it was the first smartphone that she had bought with her own salary.[1] It was also the only thing she had ever purchased *just for herself* with her salary.

Following her father's unemployment, Sheela had, along with her mother, taken on the responsibility of a 'breadwinner'. She handed over all of her salary (at the time INR 7,000 per month) to her mother for household expenses, supplementing the income her mother earned as a domestic worker. If and when there was money left, Sheela got some 'pocket money' from her mother. It was this money that she had saved and bought herself a phone with. Although she had seemingly become part of Digital India's[2] growing

Figure 4.1 A Gramin Seva minivan parked by the roadside
Source: Photograph by the author.

population of smartphone users, the smartphone had not come easily to
Sheela:

> I'm so scared of losing it; this is why I don't go on the bus. Last time I
> went on the bus, one girl's phone was stolen, another one's purse was
> stolen…. She started crying and I just got scared…. It is scary; we buy
> phones with such hard work, putting small amounts of money together,
> can't let it get stolen….

Sheela's anxiety about her phone represents broader anxiety about how young
women spend their money. Like Sheela, most women had financial agency
over only a small part of their income. Their salaries, either completely or in
large part, went to the family, where they were used for household expenses, to
pay back loans or to pay for younger siblings' education. In this apportioning
of their income, women were able to either retain or reclaim some money for
themselves. The ways in which women assessed these expenditures reflected

their sense of their place in the world and, in particular, their sense of 'class'. While the women largely agreed that middle class was not a desirable position, their understandings of what makes someone 'middle class' varied. For Sheela, buying the smartphone was a signal of upward mobility: 'We need things at home, and we never had them, so I had decided after class 12, I would definitely do a job for myself.' But there was little she was able to buy beyond the smartphone to transcend her family status. She wanted to enrol in college, even if only through distance learning, but she could not afford it. It was a toss between her higher education and her siblings' school education, and she chose the latter: 'I don't want what happened with me to happen with everyone else.'

This sense of responsibility that women had was, according to Ranjini, an indication of their middle-class status:

> In *middle class*, we place more value on family and traditions; we fulfil our responsibilities. *Hi-fi* people don't care about their parents; *middle class* people work according to their parents. I don't do anything against my parents' wishes. Sometimes I feel like it, like I want to go out; I see people in my job doing all of that. But then I think of my parents, I can't say that, so I keep my feeling to myself.

While Ranjini preferred not indulging in expenses that her parents might think frivolous, other women were less conforming. Chandni spent part of her income on pizzas and make-up, expenditures that signalled her belonging in the global economy. She told me, 'I belong from a small ... *middle class* family, but my family's thinking is not this way', referring to the freedoms she was afforded by them. Unlike many of her friends, Chandni had very few restrictions on where she went, who she met, how long she stayed out and, importantly, what she spent her money on. Other women also qualified their families and themselves as 'middle class, but not middle class', but never as 'hi-fi' or 'high class'. They did so not on the basis of how much money they had but on the basis of how the money was spent and, importantly, how much freedom they were afforded to pursue lifestyles that their parents were unfamiliar with. This link between consumption, associated behaviours and attitudes, and class, which other scholars have noted too (Lukose 2009; Osella and Osella 1999), was constantly under negotiation. And these negotiations were deeply gendered since men had autonomy over their incomes and their lifestyles, with families accepting that their contributions would be unreliable at best.

Women's incomes disrupted the norm of the male breadwinner, as well as inculcated them into new urban consumption practices (Lukose 2009) that their parents were unfamiliar with and often disapproved of. But the women also reflected on the inconsequentiality of their incomes and consumption, expressing frustration about not being able to accumulate savings that could enable more substantial expenditures, such as property. As such, while literature on youth consumption largely focuses on transient fashion, young women demonstrate simultaneous 'youthful orientation towards transience' and 'a mature demeanour directed towards achievement of householder status' (Osella and Osella 1999). These emerging subjectivities – of consumer and breadwinner, of youthhood and maturity – are intertwined with their identification between 'middle class' and 'not middle class'. While the young women participants in this research were able to access fashion, phones and lifestyles through part of their incomes and thus make a move towards being 'not middle class', the security of income and property was largely out of reach for these urban workers, pulling them back into being middle class. This chapter explores the ways in which women spend their money and how that leads to their mid-identification with middle class.

Becoming breadwinners

Jahanvi's family thought she earned INR 6,000 per month with her café job. The remaining INR 3,000 from her salary of INR 9,000 quietly went into her bank account each month. Jahanvi laughed and claimed, 'I'm very sharp with money!' She shared this information that she had kept secret from her family as we sat together on a single bed at her home, and she bossed around her younger sisters to make tea and bring snacks for us. Jahanvi did not see a problem with duping her family; if anything, she believed she was being virtuous in doing so:

> My salary is Rs. 9,000, but I've told my family I get Rs. 6,000 because I thought with money, parents will get greedy too; they'll keep all the Rs. 9,000, and I won't get anything. I didn't have a problem lying; I was lying for myself and for my family. I've told my sisters too that my salary is Rs. 6,000.

She used these savings to help her family out occasionally. When her father needed INR 10,000 in an emergency, she withdrew money from her bank account but told him that she had borrowed it from her best friend and partner in crime, Neeraj. Jahanvi thought this was a clever solution to the problem:

> It's the family money staying in the family. I didn't tell him I was giving him the money. If he knows it's been borrowed on interest, he'll try to return it. If he knows it's mine, he'll think it's family money, no need to return it. So he gave Rs. 10,000 and the interest. So the money stayed in the family, and the problem got solved.

In this way, Jahanvi was not only able to help her father when he found himself in a difficult spot, but she also regained more money than she had shelled out – this money she knew would come in handy another time. Initially, Jahanvi's father had been completely opposed to her work. Jahanvi drew upon all the resources that she could to convince him: her mother, her best friend whom her father trusted and her cousin who lived downstairs. When all else failed, she stopped eating and cried for days. Eventually, her mother was able to crack her father; he did not give his blessing, but he reluctantly granted her permission to go to work. Jahanvi's father worked as a *press wallah*, ironing people's clothes at a small stall set up in a residential neighbourhood. Her mother assisted him in this work. Jahanvi's grandparents had done the same work too. Although the casual and informal nature of the work meant that their family did not have a stable income, they were comfortable with the work they were doing. Jahanvi's entry into service work and contribution of regular monthly income was, as such, a novelty for the family. She told me,

> When I got my first salary, I brought it home; *papa* didn't say anything, but he had some sort of shame in taking his daughter's salary. He said give it to *mummy*. But *mummy* told me after I left, he counted it 4–5 times (*laughs*). And he told her to not tell me that he'd touched the money.

Up to the point when Jahanvi brought her first salary home, her father was the primary earner, assisted in his work by Jahanvi's mother. The threat to his breadwinner status, particularly in a socially visible way – everyone in the neighbourhood could see that Jahanvi was going to work every day – was, at least initially, embarrassing. Similarly, Chandni recounted,

> *Chandni*: When I started working, my parents weren't supportive; *mamma* was still OK, but *papa* wasn't … I lied and went for the training … I started the job and told *mummy, papa* stopped talking to me…. And then when I got my first salary – I've told you my father drinks – I thought that would be the biggest gift for him, so I gave him Rs. 500 for Kingfisher. But he didn't accept it….
>
> *Me*: Why?
>
> *Chandni*: Not because it was his daughter's income but because he didn't want me to work. He said if you've been stubborn about it, you keep it to yourself.

Although Chandni's father maintained that his opposition to her working was not about shame associated with his daughter's employment, Chandni herself was conscious that she had started working in part due to his unemployment. Chandni's father eventually came around; she attributed this to her judicious use of her salary – in particular the fact that she did not keep the salary entirely for herself:

> My parents are supportive now. They saw that I'm not just floundering the money I'm earning; I never kept my own salary. I don't tell *papa*, but I give all my money to *mamma*. She's like my *bank*, my *fixed deposit*. I then get interest from her (*laughs*). I give her all the money and then take whatever I need. I tell her what I've spent on.

Like Jahanvi and Chandni, many young women handed over their salaries to their mothers to avoid embarrassment for their fathers; the mothers then distributed them into household expenses, pocket money and sometimes savings. Meeta had started working to supplement her father's income. Having faced no resistance from her father, Meeta went to him when she needed money for her own expenses:

> *Meeta*: I feel like my *papa* is [working] on his own, how will he manage. And then it's been nine months since I've been working, so now my *salary* has been *fixed*, it's important that it keeps coming through. That's what I feel.

Me: You get used to the income....

Meeta: Yes, that's it. I don't have any expenses of my own. My salary comes in my *bank*, and it goes to the family. I don't spend any of it. If I need something, I ask *papa*; he says sure, get it.

Although Jahanvi, Chandni and Meeta slightly differed in the ways in which their money was handled, they were unified in emphasising that the proper thing to do was to hand over their incomes (or at least most of their incomes) to their families. As we saw in the previous chapter, young women were keen to assert their autonomy through employment – they said they wanted to work because they get bored at home. But they were also careful to delineate their work as something that they were doing for their families, rather than just for themselves. In other words, they wanted to establish that work for them was not a selfish or frivolous enterprise. Within this dynamic, although the women were conscious of the breadwinner role they were taking on, they were careful not to assert it too much, instead positioning themselves as young consumers who get money from their parents for small expenses. This helped them to negotiate their entry and continue participation in work with their families. Thus, they articulated work simultaneously as an expression of their individuality and as an instrument for improved futures for their families. As Jahanvi said, 'I am after all working for myself and my family.'

The income of a son was, of course, not shameful for the family – that is, there was no need for families to keep the money brought in by a son under wraps. But for most families, this situation did not arise at all: young men usually did not hand over their salaries to their families; instead, they retained autonomy and control over money that they earned, even spending it on frivolous purchases, drinking and gambling as they wished. In the last chapter, we saw that Chitra had dropped out of work after being frustrated at her failed attempts to secure stable employment. Her emphasis had been on stability because when she had a salary, that amount of financial contribution was guaranteed to the family. Her elder brother was employed too, but there was no surety of his contribution since he spent it on 'drinking and all'. This does not imply that Chitra's brother did not give any financial assistance to the family, but that this was unreliable. Similarly, both of Prachi's brothers were working but, unlike Prachi and her elder sister, they did not hand over their salaries to their mother. This situation – of unreliable contributions by male members of the family and women handling household expenses among themselves – was fairly common. Pranjali identified this as the impetus for changing attitudes towards women's employment:

> You've seen what *gents* these days are like. They don't work; girls are doing it…. So nobody stops girls now; they won't just think that she'll get married, she should be able to earn a living for herself. My *mummy* says study and work for yourself; I don't want you to do anything for me; I just want you to have a *secure* life. In case there are such circumstances, you should be able to fend for yourself; you shouldn't have to come to me or anyone else.

All of Pranjali's younger siblings were, at the time, studying: her sister was pursuing an undergraduate degree and a private teachers' training course; her brothers were in classes 10 and 12. She was the only one working, supplementing her father's income. But her father's income was uncertain: 'It depends on work; sometimes he works only 15 days. He earns Rs. 500 a day, so yeah, sometimes it's 15 days, 20 days. He never works full 30 days, 20 days maximum. So around Rs. 10,000.' Her salary of INR 10,000 from working as a financial assistant in an architecture firm was, on the other hand, fixed and paid for her siblings' education. The money her father brought in was then spent on household expenses since those could be moderated, unlike the fees that needed to be paid promptly each month for Pranjali's siblings' education:

> Mine all goes into education. My sister is doing a *teaching course*. This is why I hesitate to leave my job. If I leave it, her fees will be *disturbed*. Mummy will *manage*, but then she'll have to do it on her own; I won't like that. That's the problem … I've been thinking about leaving the job, but I can only leave it if I immediately find something, otherwise it will be a problem. Her monthly fees is Rs. 2,000, that goes from my salary. She's doing NPTT [nursery primary teacher training] … she's doing this privately, when she's independent, then she can see for herself….

Pranjali was committed to seeing her younger sister complete the teacher training programme in the hope that she would then become a reliable earner for the family. It was unclear what, if anything, her brothers' education would lead to. Pranajli, like Jahanvi, had not displaced her father's income; she had only augmented it. Her family was, unlike Jahanvi's, supportive of her work, with her mother particularly urging her to become financially independent. But Pranjali still retained the illusion of partial dependence by handing the salary over to her mother for distribution to various expenses, including her personal expenses:

> Right now, there are so many expenses, I can't really save. Mummy does try, she supports a lot. I give her the *salary*. After all the expenses, she puts some money in my account. The rest is fixed; this much money has to go here and there.

Like Pranjali's mother, Deepti's mother had also encouraged her to find work: '*Mummy* says this too; she says what are we educating you for, so that you go out and earn, see the outside world.' Once Deepti started working, she admitted that she no longer wanted to sit at home or do any housework. Working at a multinational café, Deepti was earning INR 10,000 per month. She proportioned the salary, giving INR 7,000 to her family and putting the rest in her account. But she did not have any substantial savings to speak of:

> I can't save everything; I have to give something to them.... Sometimes I spend it. Like if I have to get a phone. Or if my brother needs something. It's difficult to save. We would have saved if we had our own house. We spend Rs. 8,000 on rent.... My salary goes all into rent; expenses come out of papa's salary.

Again, since Deepti's salary was fixed, it was earmarked for the fixed and essential rent payments, whereas her father's salary of INR 13,000–14,000 was used for the more flexible expenditures. Deepti's brother had also recently started working – in 'computer operating' – but she did not account for his forthcoming contributions to the upkeep of the family.

As such, money for the maintenance of the household was largely managed between the women and their mothers. Some women had faced at least initial resistance from their fathers against their employment, but their financial contributions quickly gave way. Families came to depend on the *regular* income that the women could earn by entering the new service economy that had not been available or accessible to their parents. The formal nature of their work meant that they were earning a fixed amount of money each month. This could be put towards important payments that had to be made on time, such as fees for younger siblings' education or rent. In part, some women offered, this was changing the way women's employment is viewed – with the recognition that men cannot be relied upon, women's employment was becoming more acceptable. But this acceptance seemed to be premised upon women handing over their salaries to their families, asserting the selfless nature of their work. A similar expectation did not dictate men's participation in the workforce. Nevertheless, as the following sections will show, women retained *some* autonomy over their income, generating flux of gender and class relations.

Personal expenses

When Prachi first joined the café, she was told to 'come in *office black pant, white shirt*. I had only one *black pant*, then I bought two *shirts*.' She also had to submit a medical certificate and an identity card: 'I had medical made for Rs. 200, then got Aadhaar card[3] done; there were all of these expenses.' Similarly, Sarita had to invest in new clothing when she joined work: '... here because of the job, we have to wear *pants* and *jeans*. I never used to wear these; I used to wear *suit* only.' In some cases, Chandni and Chitra shared, they were even asked to pay a 'deposit' as guarantee of their interest in the job and/or for training sessions prior to joining work. Often (but not always) these were 'fake jobs', part of the larger and elaborate economy of duping people desperate for jobs to pay for make-believe employment (Poonam 2021). Sometimes they fell into the trap; at other times they decided that these expenses could not really be justified. Sheela was recruited for a job at the airport – although the back-end data work that she was hired for was managed by a company contracted by the airport authorities, this was the closest she got to securing a coveted 'government job'. When the employers asked her to pay INR 10,000, she initially considered borrowing money from friends, but she eventually decided not to take the risk.

Besides these one-off expenses, women also needed money for transport on a running basis. As the last chapter shows, the women had come to know the city and its transport system through the need to commute to work. They admired the relatively new Delhi Metro and used it sometimes, for example, to travel to the Delhi University campus to pick up their coursework. But for daily commute, they largely relied on privately run shared transport services, such as the Gramin Seva minivan, shared autorickshaws or shared cabs. The metro was, in comparison to these services, expensive and not easily accessible; to get to the nearest metro station, they would have to get a shared autorickshaw from their neighbourhood, adding to the overall cost. Even though most women did not work very far from their homes, they still felt the pinch from the cost of commuting:[4]

> *Sheela*: I get the Gramin Seva to come here and go back in a shared *auto*. Gramin Seva runs at all times; they keep calling out 'Nehru Place, Nehru Place'. From home, I get Gramin Seva to Tigri – that's Rs. 5. From there, I get Gramin Seva to Nehru Place, so I get off here.
> *Me*: So how much do you spend on travel?
> *Sheela*: Rs. 30 daily. It's a bit much, isn't it? (*laughs*)

Aarti, who worked in Gurgaon, a suburb that has emerged as a hub for service professionals, spent more than twice that amount on her commute:

> Aarti: Rs. 80. It's at least Rs. 40–50. With metro it will be at least Rs. 100; with a cab it's Rs. 40–50 both ways. Where I went before, it was the same. Monthly, it comes to around Rs. 3,000. When we eat outside, obviously there's that expense too…. But with this job, I joined without calculating *average*. The biggest thing is they told me this is in Gurgaon, it will only be Rs. 10 to travel. I didn't know how much it would come to.
> *Me*: What do you do with the rest of your salary?
> *Aarti*: I give some to my family and keep some for myself. I can't keep it all to myself, that's why! (*laughs*)

While a large part of women's 'personal' expenses was comprised of the unavoidable costs of employment – including recruitment and training costs that employers imposed on them, the purchase of professional clothing and travel costs – part of it went towards more pleasurable expenses too. Aarti included eating out as a necessary cost of employment, alongside the cost of commuting. Similarly, Jahanvi emphasised the importance of socialising with colleagues: 'I also don't tell mummy when we have parties in the office; she'd say you can have something nice at home for Rs. 200, there all friends contributed Rs. 500, so I *swipe* my *card* too.' Chandni framed the importance of spending money on eating out with colleagues in terms of shedding middle class-ness and imbibing higher-class culture:

I didn't know what a *pizza* was, what Pizza Hut is. First time, *sir* got me to eat pizza. And then with Rohan, first time we met, with *ma'am* … I had gone with *ma'am*, *sir*, Sumna, Rahul *bhaiyya*, her *boyfriend*. Sumna had brought her car; she belongs to a good family. At that time, I was feeling quite *middle class* among all those *high class* people. I didn't even know how to say *pizza*….

Coming from a background where she had not even learned how to say 'pizza', Chandni could only afford entry into this new world through her own income. Jahanvi also felt that her parents, who had done ironing work all their lives, would not understand the need to party with co-workers. This is why Jahanvi firmly believed that although it is important to contribute one's salary towards household expenses, 'when you earn, you should have money in your hand'.

Aarti too confirmed, 'You have a different kind of right over your own income, as compared to your parents' income. You can't ask parents for money for everything.' The expense that Aarti was particularly thinking of as she said this was her boyfriend's upcoming birthday. Although she was not sure if she wanted to continue going out with him, hypothetically speaking, she said,

You know if we want to buy a gift for someone, our parents might object, why are you giving such an expensive gift for someone…. We have to make a *list* to explain everything: where you're going, what you're spending on. If it's your own money, you don't have to make *lists*….

This was something Chitra was also worried about; since she was frustratingly out of work, she was going to have to borrow money from her mother and justify the expense of buying a gift and a cake for her boyfriend's upcoming birthday. For Chandni too, there were similar relationship-related expenses:

When Rohan and I go out, we do *contribution* … I've never given Rohan many gifts. I gifted him a *collage* for our first *anniversary*. For his *birthday*, I got a *chocolate and caramel cake* for him; it was only Rs. 150, but it seemed much more expensive. He thought it was Rs. 400–500…. This time, I got him a *shirt*; I took him to buy it. He's been at the *gym*, so his size has changed….

Both Chitra and Chandni were in relationships that would be seen to be beyond their social station. Chitra's boyfriend came from an upper-caste background; she had kept the relationship secret from her family, expecting opposition to their alliance. Chandni was more open about her relationship, but she was conscious that her boyfriend came from a higher-class family and mingled with higher-class people. Chitra and Chandni might have felt the need to prove their mobility, or at least their capacity for mobility, through incurring expenses in their relationships. Chandni maintained that she would like to continue working after marriage, and she admired her boyfriend's open-mindedness in being supportive of her ambition. Learning to be tasteful from him and his friends, Chandni was keen to emphasise that she did not believe in buying cheap:

> … *as a girl*, I don't have many expenses. Cosmetics, make-up, perfume etc., I can buy in a month, and it costs quite a bit, but I use it all for the next three–four months … I don't compromise on quality with these things though; for my face, I want to use good brands….

Her younger brother, on the other hand, was not judicious at all:

> I spend on my brother too; he'll keep eating stuff here and there throughout the day, like Rs. 5–10 at a time ends up being Rs. 200 per day. But he doesn't eat properly. I think it's better to spend Rs. 300, but go to Domino's; for Rs. 60–70, you can get a *corn pizza*. But he doesn't think that way. He eats *Kurkure*, chips … I also like going to Madangiri to have *gol gappe*….

Chandni argued, using the example of her brother's spending on snacks, that it is silly to spend a lot of money on things that are cheap and not of very good quality; instead, if one spends just slightly more, they can purchase something that is exponentially better. Jahanvi concurred with this understanding and applied it to her shopping for undergarments. She said, 'Others can wear cheap [bras], like the Rs. 50 ones and be OK with them. I can't; I have an *allergy*.' This is where the money that she saved without her family's knowledge came in handy; she had started buying the INR 250 bras. With an income of her own, she was relieved that she did not have to involve her mother in this expense: 'If I tell *mummy*, she'd think I'm crazy for spending Rs. 250. She'd say, are you a rich person's spoilt brat?! And she'd tell me to try another one if I have *allergy*.' Jahanvi was, however, not 'a rich person's spoilt brat' – although she bought a bra five times the price her mother would approve of, she did so on account of her allergy. Knowing that there are much more expensive bras out there, she added, 'And it's not like I'd take anything. If someone brings me Rs. 1,000 one, I don't want that; I want my Rs. 250 one.' So, it was not about the money, and it was not even about style; it was about comfort. But, of course, it was in a way about money; Jahanvi emphasised that these expenses could only come out of one's own money: 'You know there's this sense ... I spend the money I earn, *wow* ... if I take Rs. 200 from mummy, I think, she only managed to earn Rs. 180 today.... With my own, I feel like I can spend; it feels good.'

Jahanvi did not spend her secret money only on herself. She used it to buy things for her younger sisters that they would not want to ask their parents for. She also bought things for her mother: 'I went to Madangir and bought Rajasthani bangles for INR 1,000 for her. She was very surprised and ecstatic; she asked me how come I managed to buy them when I've given my full salary to them. I said I just did, just keep them. It felt good.' At times, she assuaged her family's suspicion about the extra money she spent after seemingly handing over her full salary to them by attributing these expenses to her best friend, Neeraj: '... I splurge it with Neeraj. When we go to Vaishno Devi [a religious and tourist site], Neeraj tells my father she's responsible for me. So then they don't give me much money; they might give me INR 1,000. I take my own money, and when I come back, I return them the money they'd given me and tell them that Neeraj bore all the expenses.' In this way, Jahanvi could spend money without feeling guilty about taking money from her parents when there were always more important things that could be done with it. If anything, by saving and spending her own money, Jahanvi asserted she was contributing to her family's welfare.

Other women too established the pleasure of their 'personal' expenses by indulging not just their own but also their siblings' expenses. Pranjali told me, 'Thankfully, I don't go to the *parlour*! At least I don't have that expense.' Instead, she maintained that she spent only on things that are necessary, like commuting and education: 'My main expense is travelling, and some on books, that's it.' But she did not hesitate to buy a new phone for her youngest sister: 'I ... got a telling off at home (*laughs*). They say, you don't have money, how did you get this. But I can manage it. I'm working; I can pay it off.' In this way, in addition to making substantial contributions to their siblings' education, as the previous section details, the women also took pride in being able to spend on smaller or perhaps more inconsequential things that their younger siblings wanted, especially things that parents may not approve of. Sarita argued in favour of women's employment by highlighting that women are much more likely than men to spend on their family:

> No … I think girls should work, bear their own expenses and support their families. Boys don't support families so much, girls do more. Boys think about their own expenses, girls think we should help out…. We feel like instead of eating alone, we should take something for everyone. Boys spend money with friends; they end up spending more than their salaries.

Worrying that their expenses – on clothes, make-up, fast food, gifts for boyfriends – would be seen as frivolous or selfish, undermining their participation in employment, women constructed themselves and other women as discretionary money managers. They were aware that the market, whether for bras, cakes or shirts, is limitless, but that their money is not. They, therefore, adopted a 'reasonable' approach, buying things that were a step up from their cheapest version, maybe even resembled but were definitely not the top end of the market. They took pride in being able to use the discernment and judiciousness that they had cultivated through observation and knowledge of the world around them, particularly through work, in making these non-essential but not entirely frivolous purchases. Like Jahanvi, who asserted that she wanted her INR 250 bra, not the INR 50 one or the INR 1,000 one, Chandni also positioned herself between Domino's corn pizza (a sign of belonging in the global economy) and *gol gappe* in the Madangiri market (a sign of rootedness in and recognition of the value of the local economy). In other words, they took pride in things that were middling – not too cheap, not too expensive, but in the middle, just right. It was also important for them to ensure that people around them, including me, did not think that they were being either miserly or extravagant. They wanted to be and are consumers, but they tried to draw lines that blurred as quickly as they were drawn, between proper and improper consumption.

Money does not make class

Does money make class? The women insisted it does not, or at least it does not in itself. As the earlier sections of the chapter show – in part, women commented on the middle class-ness (or not) of their families based on how accepting they were of their employment and consequently of their financial contributions, financial autonomy and mobility. Meeta told me:

> … my family's thinking is not *middle class*…. Like, a lot of times, I hear about they are saying this and that to their daughters. That kind of thing does not happen with my family. So I think of my family's thinking as *high class*.

Chandni too emphasised, on the basis of her family's eventual acceptance of her employment and financial autonomy, that 'I belong from a small … *middle class* family, but my family's thinking is not this way.' While Meeta and Chandni were categorical in that their families are 'middle class, but not middle class', others suggested that their families were not in step with the changing social milieu. Aarti, who still maintained the pretence of an early return from work for her father, explained,

> *Mahaul* [the environment] has changed but not completely. Even with my parents … you know there are some problems in my family, and PJ's [Prachi's] family, nobody wants to talk about this … so they allow us to work but also place restrictions on that.

In this way, women argued that social attitudes towards women's employment, financial autonomy and mobility, which comprise *mahaul*, or the social fabric, are closely intertwined with class formations. Jahanvi dismissed the significance of money: 'A human being is a human being. Even in torn clothes, money doesn't make a man. Today I might not have money but tomorrow I might, that's what I tell myself.' But money still played an important role, including in terms of shaping attitudes and behaviours that the women thought signified class, and indeed in terms of *being shaped by* attitudes and behaviours that the women thought signified class.

Jahanvi's extended family lived in a three-storey house owned by them in Khanpur, adjoining Dakshinpuri in South Delhi. It did not look very different from other women's homes, but there was a big difference: most women's families lived in rented flats, with many women (as we saw in the previous discussion) paying their whole salaries of INR 8,000–10,000 into the essential expenditure of rent. Deepti rued, 'We would have saved if we had our own house. We spend Rs. 8,000 on rent…. My salary goes all into rent; expenses come out of papa's salary.' But Jahanvi contested the association between home ownership and comfort of status by pointing out that people can 'pretend to be *middle class* too. They might not be, but they still do.' She aptly used the example of expenditure on weddings: 'like spending Rs. 10 lakhs on sister's wedding'. The figure of INR 10 lakhs is not misleading. In 2021, Prachi's elder sister's wedding was arranged. Prachi's family was desperately searching for loans; Prachi asked me if I might have friends who could contribute. When I asked her what normal expenditure on such a wedding would amount to, she unblinkingly said INR 8–10 lakhs. She listed things like wedding venues, jewellery, clothes, which are more expensive than one thinks, and hence even a big sum of money does not get *that many* things. Jahanvi thought spending this much money on a wedding symbolises a higher status but that

> … because [those who] live on rent, they think they're *middle class*. And they think Jahanvi doesn't have to pay rent, in fact she gets rent, so she's not *middle class*, she's above that. But I consider myself *middle class* because we don't have much money; *papa* has to work hard and gets Rs. 100–200 every day. We buy milk and somehow manage expenses … like we don't go to the *mall*; we buy clothes only for Diwali … but somehow they think I'm better than *middle class*.

In this attempt at territorialisation of middle-class status, Jahanvi explained that her family would not be able to afford such a wedding for her. She was very clear on this with anyone who seemed interested in pursuing a romantic relationship with her:

> This guy came up to me and said, marry me, I like you. I asked him if he has a lot of money. He said why, will you only marry someone with money? I told him I'm from a *middle class family*, so if someone wants to get married at a *hotel*, I can't do it. I'd get married where 31 people are married together.…

A wedding costing INR 10 lakhs versus a mass wedding[5] was a good measure of people's status, according to Jahanvi, rather than whether they are tenants or owners. Others – specifically those who were renting, like Deepti – were, however, very clear that home ownership could make a lot of other things affordable, allowing mobility to higher-class status. The concept of 'savings' in particular was very much attached to home ownership – if they did not have to pay rent, they could save that amount of money each month, although the experience of homeowners showed that money never went spare, even when there was no rent to pay. Prachi's family owned the house they lived in, but it was in a poorer 'slum' part of the neighbourhood. With her seven-member family (parents and four siblings) living in the same house, space was always short. Her family intended to spend up to INR 10 lakhs on her elder sister's wedding, but they did not have this money at their disposal; they were hoping they would get some money back from small loans they had given out to the extended family; they were also planning to secure further loans – through friends and possibly even moneylenders since their bank loan application had not gone through – to host the kind of wedding that was expected of them.

But home ownership, if in a good area, could ensure a steady income in the form of rent. Chandni's family was living on rent and had to move because of non-payment. She quipped about their landlady: 'Some people have money, big house, they may take Rs. 5,000 from us for rent. If I have Rs. 5,000 every month for no work, I would manage very well; I'd even have *parties*. There's a way of making that work.' There was, of course, more than just a hint at the fallacy that hard work equals success: the landlady, without doing any work, was able to secure a steady income because she had, unlike most of these young women's families, access to property ownership. Yet the landlady, Chandni said, proclaimed herself to be 'poor', pressing them for rent each month: 'That made me think this is *middle class thought*.' Chandni further clarified that class is not determined by money, but by *behaviour* and *thought*. Behaviour and thought, for Chandni, were reflected in people's appearance – 'it shows with what you wear' – but she insisted that lack of money does not mean you cannot transcend your class status: '… even if you earn less, you can still care for yourself'. And we saw in the previous section that Chandni paid careful attention to her appearance, judiciously spending money on branded cosmetics to take care of herself. Alongside transient everyday consumption, Chandni also had plans to help her parents buy a flat, a 'floor'. She knew it was possible, just within reach, but she had been unable to so far because of a lack of a good or secure job, just outside her reach:

> Now me and my brother are growing up. We want things to go well in our family. I want to get a good job. I don't want my brother to work after class 12; I want him to study first. With my salary, I want to get a *floor*; these days you can get a floor for Rs. 6–7 lakhs. I can pay in instalments; if I can get a loan, I'll do that. But for that, I need a job…. With this job, I didn't feel like I could do that. So I'm still looking.

With these events jobs, I can save my money, and in one year, it could get to Rs. 1 lakh.

Unable to secure a job that would enable such savings, Chandni had turned to 'events' work, or ad hoc work, which involved working at events to promote products, such as cars, mobile phones and services like restaurants, telecoms service providers, and so on. Chandni also believed that one has to have the right aptitude to become an upwardly mobile homeowner. Her family was originally from the state of Uttarakhand, where they had a family home, but Chandni was clear that they did not have a life there. She was therefore intent on becoming a homeowner in Delhi.

Although Chandni did not mention this, for some women the urgency of buying or helping to buy a house for their family was spurred on by their impending marriages. Pranjali was keen to help her family get on the property ladder but was nervous about even articulating this desire: 'I want to get a house … don't tell anyone … that can't happen with a small salary…. Once my sister and brother start managing on their own, with time, I can do something.' She also worried,

> … but I feel like my dream of house won't be fulfilled. They [the parents] will get me married. Then in-laws won't let me do it; they'll ask me to do it for them. I worry about this all the time. I want to do this before I leave; it's not possible after marriage….

Pranjali had left the decision of her marriage to her family; all she knew was that she wanted enough time before getting married to be able to secure her family's future and hand over the responsibilities to her younger siblings. She liked working but thought that the decision about whether she would continue working after marriage would depend 'on the next family'. She further added,

> I haven't thought so much about husband and all … I want my family to come to a good level first, then I have to think about someone else's family in the future anyway … I want something good in life. Good job, good earning.

Deepti insisted that people like them, who still struggle to make ends meet, are not part of the secure middle class; rather, they are the lower middle class.

Prachi chimed in, agreeing with Deepti, and adding nuance of how money can make housing, education and everyday consumption more accessible, allowing for mobility to upper-class status:

> *Deepti*: Let me give you an example. The people who come to our cafés to drink coffee are *higher class*. If our manager says he's *middle class*, that's acceptable. His salary is Rs. 50,000; he has a car, a house, everything. Things that he needs to live, he has them. We have to do so much more to *survive*, only we know, so we can't be *middle class*. If we have money, we eat; if we don't…. We could call ourselves *lower middle class*. I guess there are people below us too, but we're definitely not proper *middle class*.
>
> *Me*: But do you think your salaries make a difference to your family situation?
>
> *Deepti*: Yes, it makes a big difference.
>
> *Prachi*: You know, even with education, we can't get the kind of education that middle class children do. With them, from the beginning, their parents will take care of everything. What can our parents do? At the most, they send us to a *government school*. They can't spend more than Rs. 10,000. It's not like they can *plan* and send us *abroad. Middle class* people can do that. *Middle class* are those who have *3 BHK* [three bedrooms, hall, kitchen].'

There was, of course, contention over the definition of 'middle class', with Jahanvi and Chandni, and many other interlocutors, using it to describe those who are not poor but not secure either, and Prachi and Deepti, in this instance, using it to describe those who can easily afford security of life. There is vast literature on the meanings of and the politics of identification with the middle class, which is possibly slightly lost in translation here, but what is more interesting in these women's narratives is the aspect of life-making: what do they value and attach to assessments of class and, importantly, mobility? Prachi highlights the intergenerational reproduction of class, which is nearly impossible to disrupt – secure middle-class parents can send their children to middle-class schools and eventually for undergraduate and postgraduate courses at top international universities. As someone who had gone 'abroad' for education and settled there, this resonated with me. The possibility of 'good' education was not on offer for these women from the very beginning since their families were still working hard to, in Deepti's words, survive. They had all received an education, but there were definitely classes of education. With private education coming at a premium, they and their families had not entertained the possibility. With constrained resources, families may be able to afford private education for only one of the children, but in all cases, this possibility of private education was reserved only for later professional training, something that would directly lead to employment and hence professional status.

In some cases, women's incomes were now contributing to putting their siblings through higher education and private training courses. Chandni insisted that she wanted her brother to continue studying after class 12 rather than try to enter work. Sheela was similarly working to ensure that her younger siblings, unlike her, stayed in education. Pranjali's sister was enrolled in a teacher training programme that was paid for out of her salary. The women hoped that this investment in their siblings' education would provide their families more secure futures. There was also, for the women themselves, movement in and out of employment and education (which I will further discuss in Chapter 6); through employment, they could afford to pay their fees without relying on their parents, who had already invested some money into their schooling and pre-employment training. But work also took away time from studying, making it difficult for them to do so consistently.

Besides the out-of-reach indicators of a secure middle class – private and international education and house ownership – women also pointed out that their families were still negotiating everyday consumption, including what food they could afford to eat. Sarita, who told me that she lived in a 'middle-class' area with *jhuggis*, or slum dwellings, said,

> *Middle class* is like … the area that we live in, the house we live in, the way we live, eat, etc. We have to think about what we can cook, it's all so expensive. Like we can't eat *chicken* all the time, we have to budget for it.

Chicken, not unlike home ownership, was also in the territory of being simultaneously just within and just outside of reach – their families could afford it, but its purchase was on special occasions only and had to involve advance financial planning.

The women were, as such, unable to completely participate in global consumption cultures. While many of them worked in cafés, in all the time I spent with them, both in their workplaces and in leisure spaces, including food courts in malls, they never had coffee. Pizzas, burgers and coke were popular, but coffee was out of the question for them. In a way, it is not surprising because café culture, as opposed to mall culture, is more inaccessible, partly due to steep coffee prices. In Café Coffee Day (CCD), an Indian café chain, at the time the cheapest coffee was of INR 135. For that amount of money, it was possible to buy a McDonald's burger, which, besides being a more popular symbol of global culture, also provides more sustenance. In addition to Deepti differentiating between 'the people who come to our cafés to drink coffee' and themselves, Chandni said, 'Some people who have money will go to nice *cafés*; those who don't won't', with the women definitely falling into the latter category. The choices that women then made in terms of spending on everyday consumption were constantly moderated by their awareness that they did not have the security of savings and home ownership that is needed to become *proper* middle class or high class.

Middling consumption

Besides physical mobility, the women's jobs offered them access to personal consumption that they could indulge in without the knowledge and/or intervention of their families. While critically reflecting on the constraints of their lives, they tentatively attempted to access the promised upward mobility through consumer culture in Delhi. A major part of their income went towards the maintenance of families, partially disrupting the norm of the male breadwinner. The young women had to strike a balance between emphasising that they work for their families – that is, their employment is not a selfish enterprise – and being careful not to assert too much financial independence, which could be embarrassing for their families and particularly their fathers.

After apportioning a large part of their salaries for the maintenance of their families, the women were able to claim, whether overtly or covertly, some money for personal expenses. Strikingly, the expenses they incurred with their 'own' money are expenses their parents did not have experience of and in many cases would not approve of. For example, while the previous generation may think smartphones are a wasteful expenditure, the young women know their uses in the modern world. But they were also careful to assert that their consumption is reasonable, judicious and moderate. As such, while they took pleasure in the consumption that had become accessible to them through their incomes, they were not entirely uncritical and aspirational global consumers, as youth have often portrayed to be. Because of their slight distance from new cultures of consumption – both in terms of unfamiliarity and unaffordability – they analysed the significance of practices for their social standing.

They indulged in 'youthful' transient consumption, which afforded them partial mobility out of middle class-ness, reflecting on the inaccessibility of the security that the high class have in the form of savings and home ownership. They expressed frustration at being unable to improve their family's circumstances through their employment, assuming responsibility for their welfare. Their emerging subjectivity as consumers was, as such, closely interlinked with them becoming providers for their families, even though they were careful not to assert the latter too much. The transformations in the roles of consumers and breadwinners alike, which the young women were at the centre of, manifested in wider transformations in gender and class relations. In this flux, the women situated themselves in the middle of 'middle class' and 'not middle class' through the ways in which they spent their salaries.

Notes

1. Although smartphones have become almost ubiquitous, particularly in urban India, there are still significant gender gaps in exclusive ownership of smartphones, with families restricting women's use of phones. Being able to buy a phone with their own income, then, offered the women a chance to use it more freely (for further discussion on gendered disparities in ownership and use of smartphones, see Iqbal 2021; Islam and Manchanda 2023; Rao and Lingam 2021).

2. 'Digital India' is the name of the Indian government's flagship programme to create a 'digitally empowered society' through digitalisation of services, including public services and financial services, and the provision of digital skilling. Young people, as the current and future workforce, are at the centre of the mission to digitalise India, which is synonymous to modernisation of India (also see Singh 2021).

3. Aadhaar card is a national identity card introduced in 2009. Over the years, it has been digitally linked to various social protection schemes. While it aimed to improve the provision of social protection by standardising identification documents, its implementation has at times resulted in the contrary. With digital infrastructure lagging in many parts of the country, particularly rural

areas, the enforced use of Aadhaar has led to the denial of services. The success of the scheme has therefore been questioned (Bhatia and Bhabha 2017).

4. While women's mobility in the city is usually discussed with reference to safety concerns, particularly those regarding sexual violence, it was obvious from these young women's narratives that economic considerations were also instrumental to their ability to access, move around and work in the city.

5. Traditionally, the bride's family is expected to bear the full cost of a wedding. As an alternative to expensive weddings, mass weddings are organised by either government or non-government agencies for those who cannot afford them.

References

Bhatia, Amiya, and Jacqueline Bhabha. 2017. 'India's Aadhaar Scheme and the Promise of Inclusive Social Protection'. *Oxford Development Studies* 45(1): 64–79. DOI: 10.1080/13600818.2016.1263726.

Iqbal, Renza. 2021. 'Gendering of Smartphone Ownership and Autonomy among Youth: Narratives from Rural India'. In *Proceedings of the 1st Virtual Conference on Implications of Information and Digital Technologies for Development, 2021.* DOI: 10.48550/arXiv.2108.09788.

Islam, Asiya, and Preeti Manchanda. 2023. 'Gender Inequalities in Digital India: A Survey on Digital Literacy, Access, and Use'. Digit Working Paper No. 5 (Digit Working Paper Series). Digital Futures at Work Research Centre, University of Sussex. DOI: 10.20919/MCUU2363.

Lukose, Ritty. 2009. *Liberalization's Children: Gender, Youth, and Consumer Citizenship in Globalizing India.* Durham, NC: Duke University Press.

Osella, Filippo, and Caroline Osella. 1999. 'From Transience to Immanence: Consumption, Life-Cycle and Social Mobility in Kerala, South India'. *Modern Asian Studies* 33(4): 989–1020. DOI: 10.1017/S0026749X99003479.

Poonam, Snigdha. 2021. 'India Has a Fake-Jobs Problem'. *The Atlantic*, January 16.

Rao, Neomi, and Lakshmi Lingam. 2021. 'Smartphones, Youth and Moral Panics: Exploring Print and Online Media Narratives in India'. *Mobile Media and Communication* 9(1): 128–48. DOI: 10.1177/2050157920922262.

Singh, Anubha. 2021. 'Whose Country Is Digital India? Unpacking Dominant Power Relations Mediated by the Digital India Campaign'. *Asiascape: Digital Asia* 8(3): 164–89. DOI: 10.1163/22142312-bja10020.

5

Heroine | Jeans

Heroine

Jahanvi liked being the only woman at work; it meant she got all the attention from her male colleagues. If a woman dropped by to ask if the café had any vacancies, she would drive them away. She did not feel threatened by them, but she would also rather not have her colleagues' attention divided. It was not that she was not sympathetic. She usually took the time to talk to the women who came enquiring about work, having been in that position herself, and if they had a lot of 'problem' at home (the kind of problems discussed in Chapter 2), she would direct them to other cafés or shops where there might be vacancies. Before working in this all-male environment, Jahanvi's first job had been in a doughnut café. Her father had been opposed to her employment, and both her parents got worried when she insisted and started going to work: 'I went to the job; they started calling me several times a day. Have you eaten? Are there girls there? Are there many boys? I told them there are both boys and girls, I'm enjoying myself!'

This was a new environment not just for Jahanvi's parents, who had worked as *press wallah*s, ironing clothes at a small stall all their lives, but for Jahanvi too. Initially, as discussed in Chapter 2, Jahanvi had felt ill equipped for entry into service work. At one of her first interviews at the mall, '*Ma'am* said talk about yourself, what have you done, are you a *graduate*. I said I could but not much. She asked me if I know *English*. I told her I do but not very well.' Not very confident in her English skills, Jahanvi decided to change tact: 'Then the next day, I went in a *black dress*.' Through her failure in initial interviews in the mall, Jahanvi managed to gather intelligence about the nature and requirements of work at the mall. She decided to wear a black dress, which was not a small change of clothes but a deliberate change of comportment that signalled her aspiration and suitability for service work. This strategy worked; while the girls in the café said there were no vacancies going, 'there was a sir at the back. He asked me to come in. He said there are no vacancies, but you have a very nice *face*, very *attractive*, maybe we can keep you. There might be *vacancy* in a month or two, but we could hire you now.'

At work, Jahanvi was expected to wear the café uniform: trousers, shirt, apron and a cap. In keeping with these expectations, Jahanvi started dressing differently even outside of work, switching from her usual Indian clothing – *salwar kameez* (tunic and trousers) – to jeans and tops. Perhaps one of the most ubiquitous symbols of globalisation, jeans signal modernity and global familiarity (Dattatreyan 2020) in new India. For women, jeans – synonymous with 'Western wear' – also signal their distance from traditional domesticity. In that, while the young women I met would wear jeans, they were aware of the radical shift they had made and also of the temporariness of this development; once married, they would be expected to wear 'traditional' clothing as a sign of maturity, seriousness and responsibility. While Jahanvi's first day at work had gone without a hitch, she was not so lucky on the second day:

> Second day at work, I cried a lot, but I didn't tell them [the parents]. I cried because some girls at work told me that I shouldn't try to be a *heroine* when I'm there. They told me I should wear my work dress from home.

At home, as the eldest sibling, Jahanvi cut an authoritative figure, but at work, rivalries emerged. For Jahnavi's colleagues, it was not just that Jahanvi was dressing up like a 'heroine', an actress, but that she was *trying to be a heroine* – in other words, trying to be someone who she was not. Further down the line, while the men at her second job were kinder, they still implied that she had been hired because of her *face*; they suggested that she could be hired as a *dummy*, a mannequin for display in the store. Jahanvi worried that her appearance would be taken to imply incompetence, as it often is with women. She worked hard at her first job to prove that 'I'm good not just by my *face* but also by my work.' She was also amicable to her manager, colleagues and customers to prove that she was a good worker. When she felt uncomfortable with a manager's advances and stopped being so amicable to him, she was fired from her job: '… four months later, they fired me because there was this one sir; I didn't talk to him nicely.'

Although Jahanvi was fired, she insisted that she chose to leave (the next chapter will discuss the wilfulness women displayed in leaving work). This was, she said, in contrast to other women who continued working at the café despite unsolicited attention from the manager. In particular, Poonam, who was 'a *hot* kind of girl, quite an *item*', was subjected to the manager's comments with sexual undertones. Jahanvi had advised Poonam to leave, reassuring her that she could get another job elsewhere. But Poonam had continued working there; Jahanvi said, 'If I heard so much, there must be other stuff he says to her. But I'm not that kind of girl.' Jahanvi was proud of having the will to quit work rather than compromise on her dignity by putting up with sexual harassment (Figure 5.1). This served, she noted, to bolster her parents' trust in her. While Jahanvi's parents were not entirely comfortable when she started wearing make-up and Western clothes for work, they eventually came to accept it when they saw that Jahanvi did not do anything 'wrong' at work.

For Jahanvi and her peers, honing their appearances was a necessary practice, alongside learning English, to enter and participate in the global and modern environment of service work. Analysis of women's investments in their appearances has often been dismissive, classifying them as women's participation in their own sexual objectification. However, there are many layers to these young women's body practices. The changes to their appearance were not just skin-deep; they went hand-in-hand with changes in their *personalities* as they became service professionals. In part, the women derived pleasure and a sense of independence from the practice of cultivating the self – this was enabled, as the previous chapter shows, by the income they earned from their participation in service work. But their self-stylisation was also riddled with anxiety, in particular about how their changed appearances are assessed by their families, in their workplaces and among their peers. There was, then, fun to be had from becoming a *heroine* – an actress can craft identities, she can be flamboyant – but a *heroine* can also be judged as fake, excessive and loose. This chapter explores how women interact with and appraise emerging body rules in service work.

Figure 5.1 A poster by Delhi Police against 'eve teasing', a euphemism for sexual harassment

Source: Photograph by the author.

Professionalising appearances

In the initial days of fieldwork, I got in touch with an NGO that runs literacy and education programmes for young girls who have dropped out of formal or school education. At the time, they had a centre in Khanpur, the neighbourhood adjoining Dakshinpuri, which I started attending. Over time, I got to know Aradhna, who was the teacher in charge of the Khanpur centre, and I developed some familiarity with the students who attended the centre regularly. On one occasion, Aradhna offered me the opportunity to speak to her students about my research. I started by describing my interest in women's participation in new service work and mentioned that I would like to meet women who are employed in malls, cafés, offices and the like. One of the students said that her elder sister, Jahanvi, worked in the Select Citywalk mall. Another one admiringly quipped, 'She wears pants and shirt to work, right?' A job in the mall, all the girls agreed, requires quite a makeover; the women of Khanpur and Dakshinpuri change their bodily comportment to become professional working women.

These changes to the comportment were actively taught at skill centres providing a range of employability trainings. Indeed, 'personality development' was an integral part of any such training, alongside computers and English speaking. At some centres, personality development was an exclusive course in itself (Gooptu 2013; Nambiar 2013). These classes, aiming to refine the way young people present themselves, focus on not only speaking English but speaking English with the 'right' accent, not only adopting Western wear and make-up but being 'classy', and not only body management but body presentation suitable for corporate environments. Prachi's sister, Priya, had pursued an employability course at one such skill centre, where she received instructions on body language:

> *Priya*: Yes, I did a *computer course*; there is a centre called Pehel. They give us *training* for *jobs*, how to behave, how to talk, what our *body language* should be, how to make *eye contact*, all of that. And *English knowledge* and *computers*.
> *Me*: So that's to prepare you for a job. Tell me a bit more about it....
> *Priya*: They do a *trial*; there's an *interview* for the six months course.... They started all of this *training*.... They told us how to behave when we go [for interviews]: you have to *wish good morning* or *good afternoon*, you have to maintain *eye contact* and look straight ahead, don't move your arms, stand perfectly, *shoulders* should be straight. And what you have to say, present it in a way that it convinces the person in front of you. If you have to sell, that's the main thing. If we can't make them understand, we can't convince them to buy.

With this training in hand – computers, English and body language – Priya had success at gaining employment at a call centre and later at an insurance company, but she was not successful in her application to work at McDonald's.

While Jahanvi had not had similar training, she was nonetheless aware that clothing, make-up and body language were quick ways to transform herself for the new world of service work. Besides putting on a 'black dress', Jahanvi also learnt how to catch potential employers' attention through make-up:

> When I was interviewed for this new job, I went with my younger sister.... When I went to her [the employer], she asked for my *résumé*, then she didn't say anything except why are you wearing this *colour* of *lipstick*. I said because I like it. She said she'd seen me the day before as well when I was wearing *orange lipstick*, today I'm wearing *baby pink*, why? I said because I like this one (*laughs*). She said why so *dark*? So, in my mind, I kept thinking, what is this *interview*, what is she trying to guess by my *lipstick colour*. I wasn't entirely sure how to respond. Maybe she expected me to say I've done this for the *interview*.

Jahanvi took this as confirmation that she was moving in the right direction for entry and belonging in the world of service work. Although she was unsure about whether she managed to satisfy the interviewer with her responses, she was nevertheless pleased to learn that her make-up had made her noticeable. Importantly, this transformation of comportment could be undertaken fairly quickly (although not without costs, which I will further discuss in this chapter), in contrast to the rather long period of time that Jahanvi would have had to invest in getting her English fluency up to the mark. While, as we saw in Chapter 2, spoken English is a key requirement for entry into service employment, Jahanvi found a way around it by cultivating and emphasising her professional appearance.

Jahanvi effected a change in her appearance to facilitate entry into service employment, but the process did not stop there. In other words, appearances may be cultivated to enter services, but working in services in turn cultivates appearances too. The café Prachi and Sheela worked at required them to attend 10 days of training before starting work; they were asked to wear a corporate outfit: '*Shirt, pant, black shoes, socks, belt ...*,' Prachi told me. The transition to work was then marked by the provision of branded uniforms, which included T-shirts, trousers and caps. Interestingly, contrary to the understanding that uniforms make the bodies of workers invisible (Holliday and Thompson 2001), young women experienced their bodies as hyper-visible through their uniforms. Indeed, in India, uniforms have previously been associated with jobs done predominantly by men, such as drivers and security guards. For these young women, uniforms thus signalled distinction, especially that of gender, by professionalising their appearance.[1]

Women's changed appearances spilled beyond work too. As we chatted over momos in the CR Park market after Prachi and Sheela finished work one day, Prachi repeatedly told me that she liked Western clothes (that is, jeans and T-shirts). She made other references to the 'West' too: Western films and television shows are more realistic, Western lifestyle is better because people do not interfere, Western countries are cleaner, and so on. Office workers who were not required to wear uniforms too reiterated their preference for 'Western' wear. Even though jeans and tops were ubiquitous in the lanes of Dakshinpuri, their 'newness' was evident in young women's assertions about choosing this clothing. These changes, still relatively new for Jahanvi and her peers, had implications for those around them too. While Jahanvi's father had initially had a very conservative outlook towards women's employment, Jahanvi told me that once she secured her first job and started contributing a regular income to the household, his attitude about working women, make-up and 'Western' clothes changed:

> He [my father] used to tell me off for my clothes before; he'd say wear *suit salwar*. Now he himself tells me to wear *pants* to work. Before he'd tell me off for even putting on *lip balm*; now I don't take off *make-up* when I come home from work.

Jahanvi argued that the change in her father's attitude was a response to her not doing anything 'wrong' while working at the mall. Unlike Poonam, her colleague who did not rebuff the café manager's advances, Jahanvi insisted that she knew how to maintain boundaries of propriety with male colleagues, managers and customers at work. This did not imply that she did not interact with men – indeed, this was another thing her father had come to accept, including her being picked up by male colleagues on their bikes to commute to work – but that she had only platonic friendships with them. And since Jahanvi had successfully negotiated her father's approval for her entry into employment and associated changes in her comportment, her younger sisters would not have to fight the same battles as her.

Chandni, who started her first job at the age of 16 at a call centre, told me that she only started paying attention to her appearance once she started working. The call centre 'just needed kids with good voice and good talking style'. Chandni received basic training for the role: 'They just told us how to talk … *Hello, I'm Nishi; I'm calling from* … I had to change my name because Chandni is too long …'. Chandni might have changed her name for the call centre, but she assured me that very little else changed in the early days of her work there. Describing her appearance as that of a 'village-type girl', she told me that the Chandni I was seeing that day was very different from the Chandni of a few years ago: 'You'd say, who is this village-type girl, my hair would be sticky. My face was fair, but I used to go with oil on my face. I thought I could avoid harassment by boys if I looked ugly.' But things slowly started shifting, particularly after she started going out with her then boyfriend, who worked at the same call centre:

> I hated boys before. *My personality now and before is very different.* Rohan used to say what kind of girl is she; his friend would say, 'You should see her after she takes a bath, she's really fair, she deliberately looks like this.' I didn't like it at that time; he used to *irritate* me.

Despite the initial irritation, he eventually grew on her, and they started dating, which, for Chandni, although not exactly a turning point, was an opening of a window into a different world.

Rohan came from a well-to-do family; in Chapter 3, we saw his family had bought a Tata Nano car, a clear symbol of upward mobility. Unlike Chandni, Rohan was studying in a 'regular' college. When she went to the college with him, she noticed the girls there: '… you know, *I can't believe*, I saw their *shorts*, their *legs*, their *face*, they're so *cute!*' While not completely consciously, by being exposed to these other worlds through her employment and romantic relationship, Chandni started emulating these 'cute' college girls, effecting a transformation from the 'village-type' girl that she had been. In part, as we saw in the previous chapter, this was enabled by her income; even when she was doing only ad hoc 'events' jobs, she felt confident that '*cosmetics, make-up, perfume* etc., I can buy in a month, and it costs quite a bit, but I use it all for the next three to four months. I don't compromise on *quality* with these things though; for my *face*, I want to use good *brands*.' In this transformation, she was encouraged by her boyfriend: 'He [my boyfriend] just comments on my look a bit. He says I wear bad *colour combinations*; he wants me to wear better clothes.' But, importantly, Chandni's transformation was not to secure her romantic relationship; rather, it was aimed towards progress as a professional, prompted by her desire to fit into a world that she did not completely belong in. Chandni's boyfriend's remarks, she believed, were only well meaning and conducive to her future aspirations: '... after marriage too, he wants me to work. And I really like that.' In this way, Chandni articulated a mutual relationship between her changed appearance and work: her income provided her access to this new image, and this new image in turn helped her become a professional woman.

While cultivating these appearances, the women commented on these changes among their friends too. Prachi took me to visit her friend Deepti in the café she worked in. Prachi had previously told me about Deepti, particularly highlighting that, unlike her, Deepti worked in a multinational café chain. The multinational milieu of her workplace, Prachi said, meant that her working conditions, including hours of work, pay and management, were better, especially contrasted to the domestic café chain she had worked at. Deepti welcomed us from behind the till and got us complimentary coffees using her staff privileges. When Deepti came up to our table to chat, Prachi took the opportunity to comment on how Deepti had changed since she joined work: she had started wearing lipstick and eyeliner. The taunt by Prachi, although seemingly about Deepti's appearance, was also about how Deepti seemed to have put on airs and was now unavailable to meet her friends. Deepti laughed off the comment and said it was Prachi who had now become too busy to meet her.

Both Jahanvi's and Chandni's critical reflections on their makeovers as well as Prachi's comment on Deepti's appearance emphasise that their re-fashioned comportment signalled changed 'personalities'. Chandni explicitly connected her changed appearance from that of a village girl to that of an urban professional woman to changes in her personality, including her inclination to pursue romantic relationships. The body work (Wolkowitz 2006) that Chandni and Jahanvi participated in was in part associated with attention from men, but it was in both cases less about being desirable to men and more about attempting to belong in certain spaces. Jahanvi wanted to be the face of the café that she was working in, and Chandni wanted to be like the college girls her boyfriend had introduced her to. Just as Jahanvi could enter service work despite her lack of English skills by cultivating her professional appearance, Chandni could emulate the young women in her boyfriend's college by wearing make-up even if she did not have the resources to enter 'regular' college education like them. In Deepti's case, subtle changes to her appearance – wearing eyeliner and lipstick – were noted by Prachi to be in keeping with her participation in the world of multinationals, that is, in the global economy. Later in the chapter, I will discuss the incongruence between different sites – home, work, leisure – that the women negotiated through their appearance. However, it is also clear from Jahanvi's, Chandni's and Deepti's accounts that subjectivities formulated at work through seemingly surface yet actually quite deep transformations are not limited to work, but seep into everyday lives outside of work too.

'B-grade' work

The centre where I had met Jahanvi's younger sister was led by Aradhna. Although Aradhna was officially the 'teacher' at the centre, her work entailed much more than that. When the centre was first established six months ago, a large part of Aradhna's work involved speaking to and encouraging families in the area to send their daughters, who had dropped out of school, to literacy classes. Through this door-to-door mobilisation, Aradhna gained extensive knowledge of the neighbourhood. She told me that men in the area are mostly self-employed as electricians, plumbers and auto drivers, while women work as domestic help and cooks in private households. The average family income was around INR 15,000 per month.[2] This job profile for women seemed to be changing though, she added, with younger women choosing new professions. Aradhna said that one can tell by the way young women dress up that they work in a mall. They wear Western clothes and make-up to look sophisticated. It is common for them to enrol in personality development classes at local training centres to learn to be 'professional'. These changes to comportment, Aradhna said, were hyper-visible in the neighbourhoods due to their newness. Aradhna was supportive of young women trying to make different lives for themselves, often, as we have seen in the case of Jahanvi in this chapter, despite their family's resistance. Aradhna was herself independent, critical and even rebellious. After the class one day, I accompanied Aradhna to a food stall, and we had a wide-ranging discussion about the neighbourhoods of Dakshinpuri and Khanpur, women's work and gender equality.

Aradhna told me she had a friend who used to work in event management, putting on 'shows' at malls. Such events often hire women to promote products and services, such as cars, telecoms service providers, SIM cards, and so on. These women, Aradhna said, are *used as bodies* – notably, not unlike 'heroines', they are dolled up with lots of make-up and wear dresses that are rented out by the event management company. They are not paid per hour but according to who performs best by attracting the most customers, pitting them against one another, so they can earn anything from very little to a substantial amount for a few hours. Aradhna was critical of this work; she said she did not like the idea of women's bodies being used to sell products or services. Chandni, who had experience doing ad hoc events and promotions work, also told me that she was wary of such work. On one occasion, she was offered an events job for a few days, but when she turned up at the venue, she disliked the environment. She discovered that it was a *B-grade event* and they had employed *B-grade girls*, implying that it was not dignified work; it explicitly sexualised women's bodies. This is not to suggest that all events and promotions work was B-grade, just that the nature of this work lent itself to suspicion. Previously, Chandni and Chitra had done such events together; there was safety in numbers, but they had struggled to claim payments from employers. While employers made promises of good money – as we saw in the previous chapter, Chandni had hoped to save enough money to put down a deposit on a flat for her family with events work – the ad hoc nature of the work meant that they had little accountability. In some cases, Chandni and Chitra chased money for months, eventually giving up. Chitra decided not to do this kind of work anymore, and Chandni became critical of it; the use of women, as Jahanvi's colleagues would say, as mannequins at these events, intertwined with issues of non-payment, led to criticism.

While women frowned upon work that explicitly used them *as bodies* – in other words, made a profit through displaying them to attract customers or clients – they also expressed disappointment about work that fell short of their expectations of professionalism. In Chapter 3, we saw how the women emphatically distanced themselves from domestic work, premised on their higher educational levels. To put it simply, the expectation was that education would lead to work that required mind and skills, rather than bodily labour. Indeed, the term 'labour' was reserved for manual work. Chitra's father was blind and long-term unemployed; her mother, she told me, worked in a bank. When I asked her what work her mother did, she briefly replied 'labour-type' work, implying she worked as a cleaner in the bank. Prachi's brother, who had dropped out of school, was similarly employed in 'peon' and 'cleaning' work. Prachi had herself focused on her studies to remove herself from her family's general situation. She found work in the café, which, although initially promising, turned out to have fallen short of the promised professionalism. She remarked, 'It was so formal in the training. *Shirt, pant, black shoes, socks, belt … I was like what the hell are you trying to do?!* It's only Rs. 7,000 salary anyway.'

The training, she suggested, created a make-believe world, not consistent with the standards at the café. When I first started frequenting the café where I met Prachi and Sheela, they would both greet me with a 'Good morning, ma'am' accompanied by smiling faces. In our numerous conversations, both asserted that they were in employment because they *wanted* to be, but as our relationship outgrew that of customer and workers, they also started expressing dissatisfaction with their work environment. After Prachi quit her job over an argument with the café manager, she remarked that she really disliked having to 'keep a *plastic smile* on the whole day'. For Prachi, the smile was plastic because it was not genuine: she did not feel like smiling at work; she was dissatisfied with her working conditions, and yet she had no choice but to present a pleasant demeanour to the customers coming into the café. In other words, there was a dissonance between how she felt and how she appeared. In the understanding proposed by Arlie Russell Hochschild (2003), Prachi was one of many service workers who, engaged in front- or people-facing work, have to perform emotions to appease consumers. Strikingly, while Jahanvi was mocked for trying to be a heroine, an actor, Prachi herself recognised and was disgruntled by being compelled into acting (Islam 2022).

To exemplify the return to their *aukat*, Prachi shared with me the strife she had had with her manager when she first started working:

> The other day the *housekeeper* didn't come. I was in the café with Sakshi. So we thought it's OK; I'll wash the dishes, no big deal. I called the *manager* to tell him; he got annoyed and said, 'What are you two girls doing there? You can do the work.' But I told him straight away, '*Sir*, I cannot do the mopping.' I've never even done cleaning at home.…

Prachi felt that the manager tried to take undue advantage of her initial enthusiasm for the work by asking her to cover for other staff. It started with Prachi and her colleague washing dishes when the housekeeper did not come. Prachi noted that there was a specific gendered element to this request, as 'girls' were expected to do the washing. But the point of resistance tellingly came for Prachi when she was asked to mop the floors. Cleaning, generally speaking and more specifically for these women, is closely intertwined with gender, class and caste relations. With connotations of 'dirt' and 'pollution', cleaning has traditionally been assigned to the lowest castes; paid domestic work, which includes cleaning work, is strongly associated with poverty; and within the home, it is almost always exclusively women who do the work of cleaning (Ray and Qayum 2009; Sen and Sengupta 2016). By securing service jobs, these women hoped to escape all of these layers of marginalisation embedded in cleaning work. There are further categorisations of cleaning work too: while the housekeeper was responsible for washing dishes and mopping the floors, another employee was hired exclusively for cleaning the toilet, work reserved for the lowest caste in India. It is then interesting to note and also telling that managers never ventured to ask the women to clean the toilets, knowing that that would be a step too far. Instead, the cleaning work that Prachi's, Chandni's and other respondents' accounts refer to included washing dishes, wiping tables and at times mopping, activities that are characteristic of domestic work done predominantly by women. This strict division of tasks highlights the significance and durability of caste in modern workplaces.

Chandni had a similar experience when she switched her workplace from a call centre to a café. She eventually quit that job for a host of reasons, but she told me that she was not satisfied with the work from the first day because it was not of her 'class':

> *Chandni*: ... I didn't know anything about the *café*. I went for the *interview*. You know, if you go for the *interview*, they do it so well, you'd think it's a really big *company*. My *interview* was all in *English*; they asked for previous six months experience. Then they slowly switched to Hindi, asked about salary expectations and working hours ... I was also thinking about benefitting the *company*, but when I joined, the work turned out to be something else. It wasn't of my *class*; I couldn't do it.
>
> *Me*: What did you not like?
>
> *Chandni*: We were serving, clearing tables ... I thought it would be *kitchen work, customer management*, till operation ... that would be fine. I didn't think it would be *servicing* too, like *hotel* work would be done by those who can't do anything else. I'm studying. *Mamma, papa*, everyone else in my family is educated.

Similar to Prachi, Chandni felt like she had been duped by the employers at the pre-employment stage – somewhat symbolically, they started the interview in English but then graduated to talking in Hindi. Contrary to

Chandni's expectations, the work at the café turned out to be 'hotel work' that was not of her 'class'. This assessment overlaps with but is also distinct from the classification of work as 'B-grade'. The B-grade work was sexually exploitative; the work that was not of Chandni's 'class' was, on the other hand, just not what Chandni and her peers felt was commensurate with their education levels. The word 'class' here plays a dual role: it distances from working class-ness; it also signifies, without aligning with a specific class category, a certain classiness. Chandni positioned the activities that were not of her class against the kind of work she expected to do: kitchen work, customer management and till operation. The 'kitchen work' in the café, it should be noted, mostly involved preparing coffee and grilling sandwiches. The 'professional' nature of this kitchen work – that the workers are provided training for – makes it distinct from the cooking that may be involved in 'unskilled' domestic work in private households. By rejecting the work of serving and clearing tables on the basis of not only her own education but also that of her family, Chandni removed herself from stigmatised manual labour.

The connotation of 'serving' in particular is an injurious one – although the highly competitive service job market is of course premised on service, the word here denotes relations of servitude. The implication is that the service of service work is distinct from the service of domestic work, which is characterised by subordination, dependency and inequality. Jahanvi took a more accommodating approach than Chandni and most of her peers when she was searching for her first job. Although she had changed her comportment (by wearing a 'black dress') to enter service work, she was also willing to clean, dust and mop to enter the world of service work. Perhaps anticipating hesitation or resistance, the 'ma'am' who formally interviewed Jahanvi told her during the interview that she would have to do some cleaning work:

The ma'am there didn't ask me much; she just checked whether I know what work I'd have to do. She said I might also have to do mopping. I said I know because that sir had also said to me that 'Today, I'm sitting on this chair with a computer and interviewing you, but I also started out like you, looking for jobs. For three years, I've mopped the floors here, made doughnuts and also attended the cash till.' He said he's telling me because I might feel awkward if I'm asked to mop, but that I shouldn't mind because who knows, tomorrow, I might be in his place interviewing someone else. That thought really struck me, and I told sir that I'm ready to do the job. He said what would you do first thing in the

> morning here. I wasn't sure, but he said what would you do anywhere,
> like in a shop. I said I'd firstly clean up, dust the tables, etc. Then he
> hired me and told me to meet ma'am. So I did give the right answer!

Tellingly, Jahanvi saw the cleaning work she would have to do to secure a job
as only transitory – one can progress by working hard from mopping floors,
as the 'sir' explained, to sitting on a chair, using a computer, interviewing
others. This progress – from cleaning to computers – was discussed often
by the women. Talking about the exhaustion that they incurred from being
on their feet all day, they imagined *computer wala kaam*, or a computer job,
to be better, more respectable and more promising work. There were other
alternative imaginations too. Jahanvi's neighbour, Soniya, who had quit her
job at a fast-food outlet to pursue fashion designing, said that the work at the
fast-food outlet had not met her expectations:

> I didn't like the work. I'm now doing a *fashion designing course*. There was
> a lot of *senior-junior* there, and we were supposed to serve customers at
> the table; are we servants who will serve at the table? It was weird.

Soniya expressed dislike for work hierarchies. She entered service work as a
professional on the basis of her higher education. She therefore expected to
work with 'colleagues', rather than be placed at the bottom of the ladder in
the café. Further, she resisted serving customers at tables – while Chandni
referred to this as 'hotel work', Soniya distanced herself from the position of
a *naukar*, or servant. Soniya hoped that she could eventually find work as a
fashion designer, where she would be her own boss.

These varied reflections by Aradhna, Chandni, Chitra and the young
students in Khanpur on emerging forms of work, particularly where women
are desirable, are emblematic of the pressures women's bodies are subjected
to in the new economy. On one hand, the bodily modifications necessitated
by employment in malls, cafés, offices and the like – changed appearance and
body language – demonstrate respectable professionalism (Otis 2011). On
the other hand, the explicit *use* of women's bodies for profit is frowned upon.
Indeed, the precarity of women's employment is betrayed by the fineness of
the line between professionalism and promiscuity. For young women, it then
becomes necessary to negotiate an 'appropriate corporeality' (Casanova 2013)
by decoding and carefully engaging with emerging body rules in order to
preserve respectability (Radhakrishnan 2011; Vijayakumar 2013).

Body management

When I met Neha, she was on a leave of absence from her job as a sales assistant in the ladies' section of the department store Shoppers Paradise, waiting for redeployment to its Noida branch. Neha was about to get engaged, and her future husband lived with his family in Badarpur, close to Noida. Neha was pleased that the family was open-minded enough to not object to her working after marriage. This was important for Neha because she had invested time and effort into her education as well as learning 'how to handle customers' by 'dealing with them nicely'. She had also received training on the shop floor: 'There was this girl, she would tell me, when customers would come in … how to talk to customers politely … all of this.' Besides her job, Neha was also very interested in fashion designing; she had done a sewing course and still practised her sewing skills sometimes by making *filmy designs* like '*hearts* and *stars* … or *diamond* in the *back*' of her *kurti*s (tunics). She liked dressing up in her own creations as well as clothes she bought from the market. While her parents did not have any issues with her conduct, she was conscious that their neighbours had raised suspicion:

> That happens a lot. You get dressed, you go out in *jeans* and *top*, see the girl is roaming around … Nobody looks at themselves. If our parents don't have a *problem*, then why do you have a *problem*? But then I don't care either … Like when I used to come here for the *job*. People would say their girl is going out, she's started doing a *job*, she comes back so late at night, wonder what the area is like, she comes through lonely roads … all of these *comments* would start. And even when we'd shower and get ready, for a *party* or something, even a little *make-up*, they'd say their girls are going out like this.

Although Neha asserted that she did not care, the other young women felt anxious about their remodelled appearances even as they derived pleasure from them. When Prachi and Sheela could spend time with me after work, they invited me to stay in the café as they finished their shifts and changed out of their work clothes. There were no changing rooms in the café, so they had to cram themselves and their bags into the small toilet to dress to step out. Usually dressed in jeans and tops, Prachi and Sheela shared that they changed out of their uniforms because they did not like walking in their own neighbourhoods in work clothes that, while affording them a professional appearance, might nevertheless invite judgement from neighbours. Jahanvi's colleagues had explicitly told her to stop trying to be a 'heroine', but the women were conscious that even when the jibe was not explicit, people were drawing inferences about their class and character based on their appearances. They felt anxious that they would be either *seen* or *found* to be faking it – that is, people would either mock or be (momentarily) duped by their professional and modern appearance. This anxiety was underpinned by sexual politics regarding women's bodies, particularly amidst socio-economic change. The women worried that by aligning themselves with modernity through their clothes, make-up and body language, they were signalling sexual willingness and availability, even if it was not always expressed explicitly in these terms. Recent ethnographic studies with young men in Delhi – particularly Ethiraj Gabriel Dattatreyan's (2020) research with hip hop artists and Shannon Philip's (2022) research with middle-class men in urban spaces – show a focus on bodies and bodily cultivation among young men too, but they do not express sexual vulnerability through their bodily changes as women do.

It is perhaps for this reason that in romantic or potentially romantic relationships, women felt the need to come clean about who they *really* are. Chandni suggested that her appearance set her apart from other girls in the neighbourhood; she worried that she could be perceived as dressing up to deceive people. She decided to talk to her boyfriend about her family background:

> I told him [my boyfriend] everything about me, where I come from, where I belong to … I thought he might think the girl looks *smart*, her father might have a lot of money. I told him not to go by my looks. He used to take me out in his *car* and all.…

Similarly, when a young man approached Jahanvi with a marriage proposal, she responded by telling him, 'I'm from a *middle class family*, so if someone wants to get married at a *hotel*, I can't do it. I'd get married where 31 people are married together.' In romantic or potentially romantic relationships, as such, women were conscious that their changed appearance meant that their class backgrounds were not immediately apparent. Yet the material implications of their class backgrounds were persistent and could become apparent over time, thus generating the need to divulge their 'real' selves. So in 'new' interactions at and through workplaces, the women worried that they might be passing too well as urban professionals; in 'old' interactions – at home and in their neighbourhoods – they worried that they would not pass as professionals and that instead they would be seen to be involved in demeaning work.

Importantly, while women effected body changes for and through work, they were contested at work too; women had to carefully toe the line between professionalism and promiscuity to ward off sexual harassment from colleagues, managers and customers. Deepti had gone through training and transformation processes as other women – learning new body vocabulary, gaining fluency in English and putting on make-up for her employment at the multinational café. In the café, she said, she was wary of 'old sleazy men' and 'druggies' who tried to touch the girls when they served them. She described managing this by establishing distance from them literally by positioning her body in a way such that they could not reach her. The management of sexual harassment was more difficult when perpetrated by managers and colleagues. Some workers reported leaving work because they did not want to make a 'big issue' out of it, fearing that their parents would stop them from going to work completely. Chandni shared her and Chitra's experience of working at the call centre:

> *Call centres* are bad that way, especially smaller ones…. Both Chitra and I went together. We used to protect each other; we used to protect Pooja too. She was very naive. This guy at the office pulled on the tassel of her *kurti* one day. I wasn't in the office that day. Chitra told me. So the next day we picked a fight in the office….

Jahanvi also reported that her male colleagues spoke suggestively about women workers, evaluating their (sexual) worth in money, but Jahanvi asserted that she was spared these insults because she behaved responsibly at work. Her navigation between enjoying the attention of men and keeping them at a distance to avoid sexual harassment reflects the tensions inherent in women's body work. While sexual harassment appeared to be a common reason for women leaving work, which had implications for their progression, the women did not necessarily name it as such. Instead, they reflected on how their bodies – the tassel of a *kurti*, the bodily positioning when serving coffee, sitting too close to the manager – could send wrong signals and how they had to be responsible for managing this themselves.

This was then the work of 'body management' – practices through which women negotiate body rules in service work, akin to Hochschild's 'emotion management' (Hochschild 1979). Priya's list of correct body postures, Jahanvi's decision to wear a black dress and Chandni's indulgence in make-up are all *deliberate* actions that young women adopt for and through their employment in service work. While the young girls at the literacy classes in Khanpur admiringly noted that women who work in a mall wear pants and shirts, such changes were constantly at threat of being read as promiscuous rather than professional by families and neighbours as well as by colleagues, managers and customers at work. While other scholars note similar transformations from home to work (Johri and Menon 2014; Patel 2010), it is noteworthy that women did not simply accept different rules at different sites. Although Sheela changed out of work clothes when going back home, she took a defiant stance (similar to Neha's attitude of not caring) when it came to wearing jeans, even though the neighbours and her family frowned upon it: 'In our family, no one does a job. Girls are not allowed to go outside; they can't wear jeans. But when no one cared for me, no one cared for my studies, why should I care for anyone? I'll do what I want to.' Her employment allowed her to take this defiant stance, revealing the intricate ways in which work identities are not confined to work but interact with various aspects of women's lives.

Middling makeovers

Building on the discussion of consumption in the previous chapter, this chapter examines the boundaries between propriety and impropriety that the young women navigate through their bodies. The women's reflections on their bodily transformations, particularly on the process of embodying professional service work through body language, uniforms, clothes and make-up, placed the body at the centre of negotiations with emerging subjectivities. Modelling themselves as service professionals through their appearances was both a prerequisite to and a consequence of their entry into the new economy. In part, women derived pleasure from self-stylisation, asserting it as a choice. However, such remodelling was fraught with anxiety: while cultivating urban sophistication at work, they had to simultaneously dissociate themselves from urban promiscuity. In particular, they worried that their urban sophistication would be caught out as fake, especially in terms of class – that is, people would find out that they were middle class, even if they signalled not-middle-class-ness or high-classness through their professional appearances. Their bodies were, as such, a site of the making, unmaking and remaking of class and gender relations.

Since the women undertook bodily transformations deliberately, they appraised these transformations in themselves. Similar to surface-versus-deep acting of emotions, women reviewed their body transformation as surface-versus-deep embodiment: Chandni had no hesitation in stating that her *personality* had changed alongside her appearance; Jahanvi similarly noted an improvement in her confidence; while Priya was conscious that she was not (yet) entirely the person she was trying to signal through learnt body language. While undertaking the process of adapting to service work, the women identified these body rules as a mechanism of labour discipline too. In expecting the women to adapt their appearances, their workplaces exerted gendered pressure on their bodies. Interestingly, they in turn used these emerging body rules as a yardstick for assessing the professionalism of workplaces. They specifically highlighted the discrepancy between the expectations of professional appearance at work and the reality of unprofessional and exploitative working conditions. The women, then, used their professionalism, as signalled through their appearances, to resist such conditions.

As shown through the figure of the 'heroine' in this chapter, the women honed their appearances while also being rendered vulnerable through them. This led to them both embracing and distancing themselves from their bodily transformations. This distance was claimed by emphasising that their bodily transformation was strictly professional and complemented other skills they had acquired to enter service work, including learning English, customer management, computers, and so on. Yet these assertions were undermined by the double consciousness that their body transformations rendered them vulnerable, whereby customers, neighbours and even family members and peers might read their bodies differently, indeed pejoratively. In the negotiation of body rules at various sites, the women adopted a middling approach to their makeovers, both embracing and repudiating them.

Notes

1. This is reminiscent of Arlie Russell Hochschild's (1979) use of a quote from Goffman (1974) – 'When they issue uniforms, they issue skins' – to which she adds, 'and two inches of flesh'.
2. This was welcome information since I had struggled to find demographic statistics at the neighbourhood level for Delhi.

References

Casanova, Erynn Masi de. 2013. 'Embodied Inequality'. *Gender and Society* 27(4): 561–85. DOI: 10.1177/0891243213483895.

Dattatreyan, Ethiraj Gabriel. 2020. *The Globally Familiar: Digital Hip Hop, Masculinity, and Urban Space in Delhi*. Durham, NC: Duke University Press.

Gooptu, Nandini (ed.). 2013. *Enterprise Culture in Neoliberal India*. New York, NY: Routledge.

Hochschild, Arlie Russell. 1979. 'Emotion Work, Feeling Rules, and Social Structure'. *American Journal of Sociology* 85(3): 551–75.

———. 2003. *The Managed Heart: Commercialization of Human Feeling*. Berkeley, CA: University of California Press.

Holliday, Ruth, and Grant Thompson. 2001. 'A Body of Work'. In *Contested Bodies*, edited by R. Holliday and J. Hassard, 117–33. London: Routledge.

Islam, Asiya. 2022. 'Plastic Bodies: Women Workers and Emerging Body Rules in Service Work in Urban India'. *Gender and Society* 36(3): 422–44. DOI: 10.1177/08912432221089637.

Johri, Rachana, and Krishna Menon. 2014. 'Daily Border Crossings: Negotiations of Gender, Body and Subjectivity in the Lives of Women Workers in Urban Malls'. *Cultural Encounters, Conflicts, and Resolutions: A Journal of Border Studies* 1(1): 1–24.

Nambiar, Divya. 2013. 'Creating Enterprising Subjects through Skill Development: The Network State, Network Enterprises, and Youth Aspirations in India'. In *Enterprise Culture in Neoliberal India: Studies in Youth, Class, Work and Media*, edited by N. Gooptu, 57–72. Oxford: Routledge.

Otis, Eileen. 2011. *Markets and Bodies: Women, Service Work, and the Making of Inequality in China*. Redwood City, CA: Stanford University Press.

Patel, Reena. 2010. *Working the Night Shift: Women in India's Call Center Industry*. Redwood City, CA: Stanford University Press.

Philip, Shannon. 2022. *Becoming Young Men in a New India: Masculinities, Gender Relations and Violence in the Postcolony*. New Delhi: Cambridge University Press.

Radhakrishnan, Smitha. 2011. 'Gender, the IT Revolution and the Making of a Middle-Class India'. In *Elite and Everyman: The Cultural Politics of the Indian Middle Classes*, edited by A. Baviskar and R. Ray, 193–219. Delhi: Routledge.

Ray, Raka, and Seemin Qayum. 2009. *Cultures of Servitude: Modernity, Domesticity, and Class in India*. Redwood City, CA: Stanford University Press.

Sen, Samita, and Nilanjana Sengupta. 2016. *Domestic Days: Women, Work, and Politics in Contemporary Kolkata*. New Delhi: Oxford University Press.

Vijayakumar, Gowri. 2013. "'I'll Be Like Water'". *Gender and Society* 27(6): 777–98. DOI: 10.1177/0891243213499445.

Wolkowitz, Carol. 2006. *Bodies at Work*. London: Sage Publications.

6

Working | Job

Working

Chitra and Chandni had found their first job together, moved on to a second job together, worked separately for a while and were, at the time I met them, doing ad hoc work and looking for a *permanent job* together. A few days after her elder sister got engaged, I met Chitra at Select Citywalk. Both Chitra and Chandni were upset; earlier that day, they had travelled to collect payment for a few days' work that they had done previously. They had managed to get INR 500 but would have to go again to claim the rest of the payment. Chitra was particularly upset because on account of this running around, she had been unable to attend training for a new temporary job that her boyfriend had suggested to her. She felt like she was caught in between – chasing payments was necessary, but it was proving to be a barrier to finding another job.

As we sat outside the mall, basking in the winter sun, Chitra expressed urgency about the need to secure stable employment. In Chitra's family, resources were stretched. She was approaching the final year of her BA programme; she needed support with her studies but did not want to ask her mother for money for private tuition classes: '[If] … I could get a job this month, I could join *tuition* according to the *timing*.' Her father was unable to work on account of being blind. Her mother was working in a bank and a few small offices, doing *labour-type* work, scraping together INR 10,000–11,000 per month. Her brother was working as a driver for a *madam*, earning a similar amount, but he did not contribute a regular amount to the family, instead using the money as he wished for his 'drinking and all'. Two of her elder sisters were married and had their own households, but her eldest sister, who lived in a village, had sent her son to live in Delhi with Chitra and her family so he could have better education opportunities. The second sister was, at the time, a *housewife*, bringing up two young children; her husband did a *job normally*, helping out in a shop in Malviya Nagar in South Delhi.

In describing the occupations of her family members, Chitra used various terms for work (Arendt 1998 [1958]; Parry 2013): *labour-type* work to refer to the cleaning work her mother did, *normal* work to refer to the low-paid work her brother-in-law did and *job* to refer to professional service work that she had done in the past. A 'job', like other objects of globalisation, has symbolic significance. On the basis of their education, the women rejected becoming housewives (as seen in Chapters 2 and 3) and doing labour-type work (as seen partly in Chapter 5), instead seeking emerging jobs in the global economy. Chitra also distinguished herself as *working* from her elder sisters, who were both housewives. She added that she now wanted a *permanent job*, a stable job in contrast to the ad hoc work she and Chandni had been doing, to ensure regular income. Chitra was also keen on this because she was conscious that in the absence of regular work and studies, her family would pressure her to marry. She wanted to delay discussions about her marriage; she was already in a committed relationship that she feared her family would oppose because her boyfriend was from a higher caste.

Chitra's quest for employment was, as such, imbricated in relations of familial interdependence, in assertions of autonomy and in claims to social distinction, particularly through the *type* of work she was seeking. However, for the most part of my fieldwork, Chitra was in between jobs; she had previously worked in a call centre and a café, as well as had done ad hoc 'calling' and 'promotions' work: 'Both Chandni and I are roaming around, without any *job*. Sometimes we get it, sometimes we don't get it ... sometimes we get something.' A permanent job proved elusive, and eventually Chitra decided to give up on the job search, leaving Chandni alone. Upset with Chitra, Chandni commented, 'Once this love runs out, Chitra will just be another *housewife*', inferring that lacking employment, Chitra would naturally get married and get absorbed into domesticity.

And yet Chandni had herself quit work several times. When she quit work from the café, Prachi told me, supportive of Chandni's decision, 'She asked for time off but was refused. We're not the kind of people who would back down because we only ask for what we should get, what we know is right. *How can you expect a person to work for seven days?*' Chandni reiterated this sentiment while talking to me later, explaining that managers assumed that their families had financial problems and therefore they were 'working' and willing to be exploited. But they wanted to reject this assumption and confront their managers: 'Just because we are *working* should not mean they can say whatever they want to us.' Many women resigned from work wilfully to challenge their exploitation. As women moved in and out of employment, they used the term 'working' as an identifier, not as a verb. *Working* is a gendered subjectivity in diametric opposition to 'housewife' (Chitra wanted to *be* working so she could avoid discussion about her impending marriage and domesticity). But *working* can also be the premise for women's vulnerability and exploitation in the job market.

These young women's decisions about work – and quitting work – as such were enmeshed in the complex dynamics of precarious work and interdependence, gender and class relations and subject formation. A growing body of scholarship enquires into 'refusal of work' as a mechanism of protest or micro-resistance (Ferguson 2015; Ngai 2005; Scott 1985) against precarious working conditions. These women similarly deployed impulsive resignations – walking out of the door to not return the next day – as a way to negotiate the power imbalance with their managers. This power imbalance was not simply about work hierarchies but also about hierarchies of class and gender, as the chapter will show. In this entry into and exit from work, the women also negotiated their subjective positions: while temporary exit, especially if the work was not particularly good, was acceptable, even desirable to challenge the stereotype of the docile working woman, a longer or more permanent exit was frowned upon, as is apparent from Chandni's disdainful comment about Chitra becoming 'just another housewife'. In other words, while the women did not want to be identified as 'working' – as women who were in work because of their families' financial vulnerability – they also definitely did not want to be housewives. In this flux, they searched for vocabulary to describe their professional pursuits. Additionally, they engaged in further education and skill training during periods of unemployment, which allowed them to maintain and further their professional identities. Chandni, for example, after becoming frustrated with her job search not yielding results, decided to focus on her studies for a while. But, importantly, this was with a view to going back into work, unlike Chitra, whose exit became more permanent in her turn to domestic life. As such, while women, similar to youth in contexts of globalisation and liberalisation, refuse work as an act of resistance, they additionally negotiate their subjectivities between 'working' and 'housewives'. This chapter explores how and when women reach breaking point, or the point at which they decide to quit work. It further understands their resignations as an affective outlet against exploitation at work as well as subjective reconfiguration, demonstrating the flux of social relations.

Government jobs

I met Ranjini on her day off when she was briefly visiting her workplace – a fast-food chain – to pick up the cheque for her latest salary. Ranjini's father was at the time working as a driver, her mother worked as a sales assistant in a shopping mall, while her younger brothers were still in school. While working full time – on shifts that were usually 10 hours long – Ranjini was also pursuing a Bachelor of Commerce (BCom) degree through distance learning. Additionally, Ranjini woke up early every morning before work to practice running, high jump and long jump to prepare for the 'physical' exam of Delhi Police. She also squeezed in housework before she left for work every day. Ranjini was somewhat of an exception among her peers since she had worked at the same place for the last two years. She was aware that young women often switch jobs; commenting on this trend, she nevertheless told me that her current employment was only a holding place until she got a 'government job':

> Yes, I will [continue] for now, but it's not like I want to leave from here and work somewhere else and then leave there and work somewhere else. I'll work here until I find a *government job*. I don't want to keep changing. With changing, your *training* is useless. So I'll see if I get a *government job....*

Although, in popular narrative, Indian youth are aspiring to secure private jobs since they promise higher pay, meritocratic progression and upward mobility, in reality there is still a big demand and intense competition for public-sector, or government, jobs. Indeed, many women, similar to Ranjini, were preparing to apply for government jobs, ranging from the police force to teaching. When I asked Ranjini why she wanted to do a government job, she responded,

Ranjini: My *mummy* also wants me to do a *government job*. I said, '*Mummy*, *government* doesn't have as much *salary* as *private*.' But she says with *government* there's reliability; with *private* you never know what's going to happen next.

Me: Yes, I guess it's not stable....

Ranjini: Yes, in my family everyone is in *government job*, all my cousins, everyone. One of my sisters [cousins] is a doctor. She's gone to America; her husband is also a *doctor*, so they went abroad. My brothers are young, but other cousins are in Delhi Police, UP [Uttar Pradesh] Police. So I want to do *government job* too. I don't want them to say we're all doing *government jobs* and your children even after studying don't have *government jobs*.

Ranjini's desire for a government job was encouraged by her mother, but this desire was not mere nostalgia for the days gone by. Instead, it was produced through experiences of insecurity and precarity in low-level service work (Figure 6.1), as demonstrated by Chitra and Chandni's accounts. In addition to stability, Ranjini emphasised that a government job, as elusive as it may be, was still the golden hallmark of prestige that she wanted to achieve to make her parents' migration to the city worth it.

While government jobs were generally highly regarded, some kinds of government jobs, such as clerical or office work and teaching, were seen as particularly appropriate for women, especially in contrast to the physically demanding work that they did for long hours in cafés and shopping malls. Meeta, who was working at a café, told me her parents were keen for her to study further and find a government job. While her brothers were in 'regular' college education, Meeta was pursuing a bachelor's degree through open learning. Her brothers were set on securing government jobs – '... that's the *best*' – but Meeta had decided to find work to supplement her father's income. Her family had not opposed her employment but was keen for her to switch into the public sector:

Yes, *papa* says you should study more; brothers do too. That you should study, fill in *forms* for *government jobs*, don't do this *job*. It's not like they tell me not to work, but they want me to prepare for *government job*, it will be easier for you. Like when I get tired and go home, they say, you've worked so much, don't do it!

Figure 6.1 A leaflet advertising work in a 'five-star hotel', promising daily payments of INR 400, INR 800 and INR 1,200, as well as free meals, tips and overtime payments

Source: Photograph by the author.

Although Meeta enjoyed her work at the café, she also reflected on how tiring the work was, empathising with her family's push for the stability, respect and comfort of a government job. Like Meeta, Chandni was intent on securing a 'good job' because she wanted her brother to continue studying beyond class 12, rather than take up work in the private service sector as she had. Chandni had initially thought that a private job, even a short-term one, would enable her to take out a loan to buy a flat for her family. But she came to a realisation: 'With this job, I didn't feel like I could do that. So I'm still looking.'

Chandni had a glimmer of hope when, with Chitra, she found work at a tourism company. At the tourism company, Chandni and Chitra's work involved spotting and approaching potential customers, mainly couples, in a popular shopping mall and persuading them to come to the office (also located in the mall) for a chat. Once at the office, the couples would be seated at one of the five tables, where someone else would take over, asking them where they would like to go, what they would like from a tour, and then offering them packages. Chandni and Chitra's target was to persuade 15 couples each day to come to the office. If the customers were convinced and a sale was made, Chandni and Chitra would get an 'incentive' of INR 500. There was another related target: in a month, at least two customers they brought to the office should make a purchase worth INR 1 lakh each. Chitra told me: 'And then our salary was separate.... Salary was Rs. 12,000. With incentive ... incentive would come every three months ... so I'd get Rs. 15,000.' This was a good salary considering that their peers working in cafés were earning only between INR 7,000 and INR 12,000. But this did not last long:

> *Chitra*: Then they started halving this salary.
>
> *Me*: Why?
>
> *Chitra*: I don't know. They said they couldn't manage their *budget*. We said, what's the *office* for. You have to give us *salary*. Then we had a lot of issues. All staff quit together. Then they built a new brand. Nobody can be stopped. They said, fine, you can leave. After we left, we didn't get salary until three months later. They said why did you leave. We said if you don't pay us, what can we do?

Chandni and Chitra were tempted into this short-term work because it held promise of making money quicker. They thought they could work hard, supplementing their salaries with bonuses and incentives. But their experience showed that, first, target-based payments were hard to secure because the targets set were almost impossible to achieve, and, second, as that work was ad hoc, so was the payment. The payment could be reduced or not made at any point, which led to insecurity for these young women and their families. Chandni and Chitra lamented the money they had spent travelling to receive delayed payments for sums as small as INR 500.

While this was more commonly the case with ad hoc work – women who did 'regular' work in the private sector were assured of a monthly salary, especially where they were working for well-established chains or companies – there were still issues of non-payment of overtime work as well as a lack of security about how long the job would last. Deepti was employed in a multinational café, which Prachi believed offered better working conditions than the domestic café chain she had worked in. When Prachi and I went to visit Deepti at the café, she did not charge us for the coffee, something Prachi was impressed by because she did not have that privilege at her workplace. Boasting about it, Deepti said, 'Yeah, I told the *manager*, these are my friends, I've given them *free coffee*. He said why did you charge them for the *doughnut* then (*laughs*).' While there were such advantages to working for a multinational company, Deepti and Prachi discussed issues that were common to their workplaces:

> *Deepti*: I don't take *cash* with me anymore; it goes missing. We have to get our *cash* audited when we go to the *café*, because what if it increases. If it decreases, that's fine, you spent it somewhere. But if it's excess…. That's why you have to do entries for when you enter and when you leave.
>
> *Prachi*: This is part of the *log-in punch*…. I used to think if I *log in* early and *log out* late, I'd get some *plus* for that but nothing!
>
> *Deepti*: Yeah, you never get *overtime*, it's really bad. I don't like it. Once in a while, it's fine. But when you're getting us to do it every day, you should pay *overtime*.

Although cafés used log-in and log-out punches to monitor the time the employees spent at work, they never paid them for overtime work. Prachi asked, 'How can you expect a person to work for seven days?' but such a pattern of work was common across the types of service work these women were engaged in. Overtime work was routine, and most women worked substantial overtime hours – both additional hours during their contracted workdays as well as additional days beyond their contracted workdays. Deepti got a day off only once in ten days:

> *Me*: What do you do in your free time?
>
> *Deepti*: I have no free time! When I get a day off, I wash my *dress*, then I listen to mummy telling me off, that's afternoon. Then I sleep, then it gets to dinner time…. I get a day off in 10 days, what can I do…. In one day off, there are so many things to do…. Even my parents say, we never know when you're at home….
>
> *Prachi*: I've decided I'm not going to work where I don't get Sunday off…. I don't want to do *timepass*; I don't have time….

Prachi asserted that unlike young men (Jeffrey 2010), young women have no time to indulge in *timepass*, and by this point, Prachi had decided that work that did not provide acceptable working conditions was not worth her time. Prachi further added that as workers, they had very little value in the workplace. Deepti also shared that she felt quite dispensable in her workplace; she knew if she quit her job, the manager would find someone to replace her quickly. Prachi felt that this dispensability meant that employees did not concern themselves with efforts to retain them – in other words, efforts to inculcate loyalty. She noted,

> Once the *owner* visited the café and he should have asked us whether we like working there or not, but nobody cares. It's such a big *brand*. They show something on the front, but behind the back, it's different. I've had so much problem there, I can't face those people anymore.

A few months after I first met her, Ranjini, who was hoping to be promoted to floor manager, told me that her workplace had to shut down because of dwindling profits. Ranjini had been practising to enter coveted work with Delhi Police. After she was rendered jobless, she channelled all her efforts towards the much-preferred alternative of a government job, but this too did not work out. Her situation reveals an interesting conundrum for young workers in urban India: as public jobs are shrinking, private jobs are also not secure. Leela Fernandes (2006) notes that while it is the lack of public jobs that is often lamented, retrenchment in the private sector is a significant phenomenon. Ranjini went from hoping for a promotion and eventually entry into stable government work to not having work at all. These young women's evaluation of their work, even though regular and salaried, as insecure was, as such, accurate and informed their decisions about their exit from work.

Gendered problems

On one of my 'observation' days in the neighbourhood café where Sheela and Prachi were employed, I witnessed an area managers' meeting. Dressed in shirts and black trousers, a group of men pulled tables and chairs together to sit in a boardroom format. The café workers – with titles like 'brew master' and 'housekeeper' – were behind the counter, dressed in T-shirts and trousers.

The gender differentials in the café were stark: all the area managers around the table were men, whereas two out of three workers behind the counter were women. I made the observation to Sheela, who shrugged and responded, 'That's how it is.' She told me that there had been one or two women area managers, but it was common (and somewhat accepted) that despite the large number of women employed as waiters, cashiers and baristas in these cafés, it was mostly only men who made it to managerial positions. Sheela was one of the few respondents who lasted relatively long in her job, around 18 months. In that time, she was once awarded the 'employee of the month' recognition (for which she took home a coffee hamper) and was promoted from 'team member' to 'brew master'; this was not accompanied by a significant pay rise though. Even though Sheela had been a dedicated worker, she did not see scope for herself at the managerial table. Deepti also thought that she could not possibly make a 'career' in the café business:

> … our *seniors* won't let us progress, I've seen that here. There's a lot of *politics* in this line…. If people stop doing *politics*, there's a lot of opportunity for progressing…. In our *café*, there's just one *store manager* in South Ex who is a girl, the rest are boys.

Other café workers too had heard about one woman who had gone on to become a café manager in the South Delhi zone, but unfortunately, I never managed to find her. The women, however, did not completely blame employers for their lack of progression. They suggested that their families and the expectation to get married, have children and manage domestic responsibilities *also* held them back. Meeta expressed concerns about career progression and explained them through the 'personal problems' that working women face:

> *Meeta*: … what happens is that girls leave in the middle because of some *problem*, so they don't make it to the top.
> *Me*: Why do you think that is?
> *Meeta*: Because they do it [the work], they learn all the work as well, but then they have *problem* at home, so they quit.
> *Me*: Like what problems?
> *Meeta*: Like if they have to go somewhere, they can't leave the girl alone at home. With me as well, I'm going to have this *problem*; I don't know if I'll get time off. My family has to go to the village for a

wedding, my uncle's son, everyone will go. They came here recently, and they are pressuring us to come, so everyone will have to go. I'm the *favourite* at home, so they're saying Meeta has to come. Now I have this *tension*, whether sir will give me time off, will I have to quit the job. And I've learnt everything now, so I don't feel like leaving.'

Sarita quit work in a café after a year and a half because of low pay, to study for her exams and for unstated 'personal problems'. When I met her, she had recently joined another café, but she did not think she would stay there for very long –

Me: Will you continue here?
Sarita: I'll continue another 5–6 months. I have to go somewhere, so I'll need time off. If I can get time off, it's fine. If not, then I'll have to quit. It's important to go to the village as well. *Mummy* has *tension* about *didi*'s [elder sister's] marriage. She's been looking for a while but can't find a match, don't know what the plan is…. We have to go in May; we've booked it too….

These 'personal problems' and 'tensions' are distinctly gendered and broadly fall within the category of what Hanna Papanek (1979) calls 'status production work', or work done by women to maintain the status of families, such as training of children, preparation of feasts, religious observances, and so on. The compulsion to participate in such status production work had an impact on the women's ability to stay in employment over a longer period of time, limiting their avenues for progression. Further, although the women distanced themselves from the position of 'housewives', they were still compelled to participate in domestic and care work to a certain extent. They were also aware that as unmarried women, they could avoid some of these responsibilities, but once they got married, they would have to take on even more domestic and care work. As women caught between 'a flexible job market and less flexible societal structures affecting their lives, such as heterosexual marriage, maternity, care-work' (Betti 2016: 8), the respondents for this research noted their precarious relationship with waged labour (Federici 2006) and the precariousness of their lives beyond the workplace (Millar 2017; Nielsen and Waldrop 2014).

In the interplay of insecurity of work, instability of lives and inevitable participation in unpaid work, some women discussed operating within gendered networks of labour. That is, decisions around finding and leaving employment were made among women in households, just as money was managed by women in households. Some young women had 'relieved' their mothers of precarious employment as domestic workers and factory workers by finding 'respectable' semi-skilled service work. Deepti told me that her mother was a 'housewife'. But later in the conversation, Deepti explained that her mother had stopped working when she started her café job:

Me: What do your parents do?

Deepti: Mummy is a *housewife*. Papa works in a *private factory* … as *salesman*, I guess. He's in the *field*. Like there's a company that makes products for children, he has to deliver them to shops and get payment from them … It's in Saket.

…

Me: Was your mother never employed?

Deepti: She used to be. She left it when I started working. She used to work in a *company* [factory] too as a *checker*. Then she quit. I told her when I'm working, she doesn't need to. Somebody should stay home. My brother is young too; he goes to *school*.

It is interesting that Deepti's assessment of the 'need to work' was limited to women in the family and emerged in conjunction with the need for someone to 'stay at home'. Other young women who had replaced their mothers as the 'employed woman' in the household also confirmed this while asserting their own independence in seeking employment. Prachi's mother took up domestic work after Prachi's father was fired from his job. Her elder sister started looking after the younger siblings and, as a result, had to discontinue her education. Once they were all older, her elder sister started part-time work in a boutique, Prachi found work in a café, and her younger sister, Priya, joined a call centre. Both Prachi and Priya, unlike their elder sister, were able to finish class 12 and enrol for undergraduate degrees. With increased income coming into the household, Prachi's mother was able to leave domestic work.

This exchange of productive and reproductive labour, common among mothers and daughters, also took place between sisters. When Prachi was unable to immediately find work after quitting from the café, her younger sister, Priya, stepped up to fill in the 'employment gap' and found work in a grocery store in the mall. Similarly, Sheela, who eventually quit her job over an argument with a colleague, decided to return to studies that she had suspended, but only after her younger sister was old enough to find a job and substitute her contribution to the family income. The exchange of productive and reproductive labour should, however, not be mistaken for a paid worker being relieved of all reproductive work in the family. Instead, this exchange was continual, complex and messy. Interestingly, none of the women ever highlighted that they had quit work based on their father's or brother's employment situation (although, as discussed, they referred to fathers' unemployment as family 'problem' that might have propelled them and their mothers *into* employment). These exchanges, read alongside earlier discussions of women's identification as 'professionals' (not housewives), disrupt the assumption that women are more 'attached' to domestic and care work.

Affective resignations

When Jahanvi started her first job at a doughnut café, she wanted to be a model employee – she took pride in her ability to learn quickly and work hard. She said, before anyone knew it, she became adept at the various doughnut recipes and fillings. Although she had found this work with great effort, entered it against her father's wishes and was invested in proving herself, she lasted there only for four months. She told me that she was asked to leave because she refused to indulge the sexual advances of a manager: '… there was this one sir. I didn't talk to him nicely. He used to look at me in a way that made me very uncomfortable. But he noticed that I talked nicely to everyone else.' By Jahanvi's account, the manager took the opportunity to fire her when she turned up 10 minutes late at work one day. Initially, Jahanvi protested the unfairness of his decision: 'I said, *sir*, my *shift* starts at 10 a.m.; even if I come at 10.30 a.m., you can't make me do that. There's so much *traffic*; whether it's a *private* or a *government job*, being *late* by 10–15 minutes is allowed.' When he refused to engage, Jahanvi grew angry and told him even if he wanted her to stay now, she would not. This switch from pleading to anger seemed to have an effect because the manager then asked her if she wanted to stay. But Jahanvi refused, wrote her resignation letter and left the job. Jahanvi's account of her resignation is interesting in that although she was asked to leave the job – that is, technically 'fired' – she was keen on framing it as her decision to resign. Taking control of the situation by resigning, Jahanvi also distanced herself from other girls in the café who tolerated this particular manager's behaviour: 'I told her, Poonam, [a colleague], don't think you won't get another job…. But she's still working there…. But I'm not that kind of girl.' By establishing herself as a 'respectable' girl, Jahanvi said she was successful in finding another job:

> Where I work now, one of my colleagues used to work at my old workplace too. When I came here, he recognised my name. He said he'd heard about me; he used to work the night shift. So he then backed me. He told *ma'am* that I'm a very good girl; he explained why I'd resigned from there and said that he'd never heard any bad thing about me. He said to me one day, there are so many pretty girls around, *don't mind*, but during the *night shift* we used to talk about how we could run another business alongside donuts. Boys come because they're attracted to girls. He said they first talked about Poonam and how much men would pay for her, then the other girls, then it came to me, Jahanvi. As soon as I was mentioned, they all said, nobody can talk about Jahanvi, she's a very nice girl! With Poonam, even if she quits now, she'll still be talked about. If I hear things here, I'd quit from here. I have problems at home, but that doesn't mean I keep working there. I'll eat less for two days, but I won't tolerate that.

Acknowledging the precarity of life – the loss of income would impact her family's everyday livelihood – Jahanvi asserted that preserving dignity was more important. As noted in the previous chapter, Chandni and Chitra had faced a similar issue in their first job at the call centre: their manager sexually harassed the young women in the office, but there seemed to be no avenue to complain about him since he was the '*boss* of the *office*'. While trying to protect her colleagues, Chandni also emphasised that it is certain types of women who attract such negative attention from men:

> In front of us, he [the manager] used to watch dirty adult videos. He showed Pooja a *bikini girl*. He never showed me. You know people do this depending on what kind of a girl you are…. He always attacked Pooja….

While Chandni believed that she was clever enough to dodge the manager's sexual advances, she left this work within two months of starting it. She complained about the impossible targets that the call centre placed on the callers. So when her family suggested going to the village once she had finished her class 12 exams, she took this opportunity to quit. And since Chitra did not want to work there alone, she quit too. Chandni told me about the multiple jobs that followed this one: 'Then I joined HDFC Bank, *credit cards section*, but they never paid much attention to me; there didn't seem to be any *growth*, so I left it. Then I went to the café.' She quit the café because the manager refused to allow her some time off to celebrate her anniversary with her then boyfriend. Chandni was briefly transferred to a different branch of the café, but she lasted there only for a couple of days. Prachi reported, 'In that café, there was no lock on the washroom. She [Chandni] couldn't survive there even two days. She said there was a lot of takeaway rush there, and there were mostly boys there; she felt awkward.' Prachi herself quit because she felt the café had not delivered on the promise of professionalism when she was recruited and trained for this job. In particular, she found her colleagues unprofessional: 'I expected professionalism in their behaviour and respect; *he should behave like that*, they're the ones training us. *I back out from that; it was horrible.*' Prachi made references to a culture in which colleagues talked about her behind her back, used undignified language in her presence and passed uncouth remarks about her.

Both Prachi and Chandni quit their jobs by just not turning up the next day. Prachi reported, 'So for some time she [Chandni] hasn't been going, I haven't been going either.' That is, rather than follow the formal process of tendering a resignation and serving a notice period, the women often quit work impulsively. Further, their resignations did not specifically invoke the contractual obligations of the employer. That is, while they complained about being made to work overtime without additional payment, they did not cite this as a reason for quitting work. Instead, they articulated specific breaking points as the reason for leaving work; for instance, following an unpleasant incident at work that undermined their respect, they chose not to show up to work the next day and thereby terminated their contracts spontaneously. Prachi said she did not see much point in participating in formal workplace processes. She framed this as defiance of the expectation that 'girls who are "good" work silently'. She asserted, 'I'm not like this. I do what I think is right. I don't want to do the kind of work where I feel insulted, where I work hard and still can be told whatever.' Prachi commented on how all of them were mistreated at work because their employers knew that they came from modest backgrounds, or *chhote ghar*, pointing to the class difference between them and the managerial staff. They were also largely working under the direction of men, and she felt that that *male ego* was at play in their workplace dynamics.

In this imbrication of gender and class relations at the workplace, women expressed and asserted their resignations as wilful, emotional and impulsive. Their retrospective reflections showed that there were always multiple reasons that were varied as well as cumulative, leading to their resignations. The larger point that Prachi and Chandni were keen to make through their resignations was that they were not willing to put up with exploitative working conditions. However, these decisions about resigning were not always straightforward and easy. Deepti said that although she somewhat liked her work (and definitely did not want to sit at home), she had been thinking about quitting for a while. When I probed further, she said it was to do with the manager's behaviour:

> Like when you get told off for no mistake of yours. Or when they tell me off in front of other people. We can't react to that; I get angry. Then I think I should quit; there's no respect, no value for my work, so what's the point. But then I can quit, it doesn't impact him in any way; he'll find more staff.

Deepti felt that she was not respected by her manager; further, while this made her want to leave work, she was aware that her attempt to protest by resigning would go unnoticed. She knew very well that as a low-paid and low-level member of staff, she was replaceable. She was also not confident that she would be able to find another job immediately and contemplated the unhappy prospect of having to 'sit at home'. With a vulnerable position in the workplace, Deepti was unable to respond to her manager, even when she thought his reprimands were unfair. Further elaborating on the reasons that made her want to quit, Deepti said,

> You know he used to tell me off so much, I would feel like crying on the inside, then he'd put me in the front … I cried one day too. First off, we didn't have enough staff. Just the two of us. How much work can two people do? Then they'd come and point out mistakes, you didn't do this, you didn't do that. I didn't argue. I don't say much, I keep it inside myself, and I let it out by crying. They're going to point out mistakes in everything. I thought if I stay, I'll say something angrily. I went downstairs and started crying. When I came up, he asked, 'Have

you been crying? Oh, I'll never say anything anymore.' Then he tried to make it up to me. I told him not to do this for me.

Deepti's management of her emotions in this instance was reiterated by several women. Crying after conflicts over issues such as failure to accomplish sales targets, arriving late, taking time off or making mistakes was a common refrain. Sheela reported Chandni emerging from the toilet with 'red puffy eyes' after the manager refused her leave to celebrate her anniversary; Prachi said she cried when Sheela told her what other colleagues had been saying about her; Shipra cried when she was put in a team separate from her friend, Kirti, in a call centre. In her study of neophyte factory women in Malaysia, Aihwa Ong (2010 [1987]: 165) notes the phenomenon of women workers' emotional outbursts: '… a female office worker noted that when foremen scolded the operators, the latter were not allowed to respond but had to be "very polite".… Crying sometimes seemed the only way to seek relief from being reprimanded and to obtain pardon' (also see Ngai 2005: 165–88). While crying may seem like a fairly innocuous reaction to unfair and even hostile conditions of work, the young women were aware that this response could make their managers conscious of their behaviour without explicitly challenging them. For these young women, crying was therefore an acceptable way to express their unhappiness about being treated disrespectfully without explicitly confronting their managers, particularly since they lacked avenues for protest, such as unions, strikes and workplace disciplinary procedures.

Deepti had been considering resigning from her position, but she decided to wait because she had heard that she might get transferred to another branch of the café, where Deepti hoped she might get a better manager. She told me that a previous manager, a woman, made work much less stressful for the workers by creating a non-hierarchical work environment:

> I got a really nice *manager* in the morning shift; she was less a *manager*, more a *friend*. When we'd go in the morning, the first half an hour would be our *selfie session* (*laughs*). We'd take 50, then we'd select a few to post. We'd get ready together. She'd also scold us and get us to do work like a *manager*, but still be friendly. We didn't even notice, six months went by. Then *ma'am* left. That's when we started feeling like we're *staff*.

While the hierarchy between managers and workers was clear, young women also found themselves in conflict with colleagues at work. When

Prachi quit work from the café, apparently after getting into arguments with the manager and some of her colleagues, she commented on Sheela's continuing employment there: 'I told her I understand there's a problem at her home, but how long can we put up with this ...' Sheela, while also aware of the manager's and other colleagues' misbehaviour, seemed intent on sticking to it at the time. She eventually reached her breaking point after an argument with a new colleague, who she said came from a well-off family. The new colleague's higher-class status, Sheela felt, gave her a sense of impunity. Sheela was further hurt because no one in the café, including the manager, supported her in the argument despite her having worked there for so long. When Sheela finally quit her café job after 18 months of employment, her manager called and requested that she come back. When she did not acquiesce to his request, she got a call from the head office, who offered to transfer her to another branch of the café to resolve the conflict with her colleague. For Sheela, who had quit because she felt insulted, this was a brief moment of feeling 'valued' for her work. She accepted the offer but then decided to quit to return to studying after her younger sister found a job.

Other women had also engaged in similar negotiations following their resignations from work, which enabled them to gain an upper hand over their managers, even if only briefly. Although the young women were not indispensable, managers did seem to be affected by their exit from work. This might have been due to the costs of training new staff, but it might also be the case that a consistently high turnover of staff would have reflected badly on the managers' performance. When the women quit impetuously, the managers attempted to pacify them, although these efforts did not entail offers of higher pay. Therefore, through their resignations, the women did not seek to negotiate material gains; rather, their wilfulness to leave work helped them assert to their managers that, contrary to their manager's assumptions, they did not *need* this job. Through their resignations, the women attempted to re-establish the respectability that they perceived was continually undermined in low-end service work.

Middling strategies

The wilfulness that the women asserted in quitting work suggested that with little power and no formal channels to challenge the conditions of their employment, they saw resignations as a strategy of resistance. This is not to suggest that they managed to secure better conditions, or indeed even better employment, through their resignations, but that their resignations offered them a momentary sense of power in relation to work. As the chapter shows, many women's resignations resulted from various kinds of conflicts with managers regarding time off, work tasks, the workplace environment and sexual harassment. The women felt that the managers acted disrespectfully towards them because they believed that women (of their class) work out of necessity and therefore would be docile workers, not resistant to exploitation. Through their resignations, the women were keen to challenge this ascription. Their resignations, as such, emerged in the conflict between their and their managers' understanding of what it means to be a 'working' woman. While they expressed agency in their identification as 'working', managers ascribed them vulnerability.

While the women identified specific breaking points that led to their resignations, they situated them in the wider context of low pay, long hours and a lack of progression at work. Arguably, since they did not see a 'career' or a long-term future for themselves in their workplaces, they felt free to switch 'jobs', which were non-specialised work in a variety of emerging services. The women's resignations nevertheless had material implications for their families – that is, the loss of income was not an insignificant matter. Although their resignations were impulsive, they were not without thought. To ensure that their families did not find themselves in financial hardship, they usually only quit work when another member of the family, usually a younger sister, found or was likely to be able to find a job. Further, in this exchange of labour that allowed their impulsive resignations, young women participated in a broad range of (non-income generating) 'work' beyond paid employment, including further study and skill training for employability, unpaid housework and family obligations to maintain status and improve future prospects. Their movement in and out of employment finds resonance with the broader phenomenon of the multiplication of livelihood strategies among young people navigating precarious socio-economic conditions (Ferguson and Li 2018; Scully 2016).

As the previous chapters in the book show, the young women repeatedly emphasised that they did not want to become 'housewives' (Islam 2020). In other words, they did not leave employment because of 'attachment' to, or preference for, reproductive labour, as has been historically argued for women (Betti 2016; Sen 1999). But they also did not want to be seen as 'working' women who would silently allow their exploitation. While it may seem counterintuitive that the women removed themselves from work to establish themselves as respectable working women, they asserted that this was not a final exit from employment, only resignation from a job. They engaged in other related activities, including education, skill training and, indeed, search for employment to maintain their identification as professionals, not housewives. As such, their resignations constituted a middling strategy for their mid-identification with *working* – they quit work to prove that they were agentic rather than vulnerable working women.

References

Arendt, Hannah. 1998 (1958). *The Human Condition*. Chicago, IL: University of Chicago Press.

Betti, Eloisa. 2016. 'Gender and Precarious Labor in a Historical Perspective: Italian Women and Precarious Work between Fordism and Post-Fordism'. *International Labor and Working-Class History* 89: 64–83. DOI: 10.1017/S0147547915000356.

Federici, Silvia. 2006. 'Precarious Labor: A Feminist Viewpoint'. Lecture delivered at Bluestockings Radical Bookstore, New York City, NY, as part of the 'This is Forever: From Inquiry to Refusal Discussion' series, 28 October 2006. https://inthemiddleofthewhirlwind.wordpress.com/precarious-labor-a-feminist-viewpoint. Accessed 24 May 2024..

Ferguson, James. 2015. *Give a Man a Fish: Reflections on the New Politics of Distribution*. Durham (NC) and London: Duke University Press.

Ferguson, James, and Tania Murray Li. 2018. 'Beyond the "Proper Job:" Political-Economic Analysis after the Century of Labouring Man'. Working Paper 51, Institute for Poverty, Land and Agrarian Studies (PLAAS), University of the Western Cape, Cape Town.

Fernandes, Leela. 2006. *India's New Middle Class: Democratic Politics in an Era of Economic Reform*. Minneapolis (MN) and London: University of Minnesota Press.

Islam, Asiya. 2020. '"It Gets Really Boring If You Stay at Home": Women, Work and Temporalities in Urban India'. *Sociology* 54(5): 867–82. DOI: 10.1177/0038038520934995.

Jeffrey, Craig. 2010. *Timepass: Youth, Class, and the Politics of Waiting in India*. Redwood City, CA: Stanford University Press.

Millar, Kathleen M. 2017. 'Toward a Critical Politics of Precarity'. *Sociology Compass* 11(6): 1–11. DOI: 10.1111/soc4.12483.

Ngai, Pun. 2005. *Made in China: Women Factory Workers in a Global Workplace.* Durham (NC) and London: Duke University Press.

Nielsen, Kenneth Bo, and Anne Waldrop (eds.). 2014. *Women, Gender and Everyday Social Transformation in India.* London and New York (NY): Anthem Press.

Ong, Aihwa. 2010 (1987). *Spirits of Resistance and Capitalist Discipline.* Second. Albany, NY: SUNY Press.

Papanek, Hanna. 1979. 'Family Status Production: The "Work" and "Non-Work" of Women'. *Signs: Journal of Women in Culture and Society* 4(4): 775–81.

Parry, Jonathan. 2013. 'Company and Contract Labour in a Central Indian Steel Plant'. *Economy and Society* 42(3): 348–74. DOI: 10.1080/03085147.2013.772761.

Scott, James C. 1985. *Weapons of the Weak: Everyday Forms of Peasant Resistance.* New Haven (CT) and London: Yale University Press.

Scully, Ben. 2016. 'From the Shop Floor to the Kitchen Table: The Shifting Centre of Precarious Workers' Politics in South Africa'. *Review of African Political Economy* 43(148): 295–311. DOI: 10.1080/03056244.2015.1085378.

Sen, Samita. 1999. *Women and Labour in Late Colonial India: The Bengal Jute Industry.* Cambridge, UK: Cambridge University Press.

7

Middle lives

A woman's job

As I was wrapping up what later turned out to be only the first leg of my fieldwork, I encountered the feminist discomforts that I note in Chapter 1 – while my research was, in part, motivated by the debates on the decline in women's participation in the workforce, I had largely spoken only to women who were employed or in between jobs. A friend told me her family's maid lived in Dakshinpuri, my research participants' neighbourhood, and knew women who were not in employment. I took up the kind offer and met up with Rama in her one-bedroom home on the top floor of a three-storey brick building in Dakshinpuri. She introduced me to her son and proudly told me that he was excellent at math. She shared some of her life story too – originally from Calcutta (West Bengal), Rama had separated from her husband and lived in Delhi with her son, earning an income through domestic work. Rama's employment – as a maid in several households – was, as several young women who I had been spending my time with had asserted, driven by necessity and a lack of education and skills. For Rama though, employment enabled her independence and improved prospects for her son's future. She discussed, but did not dwell on, the difficult circumstances that had led her to seek such employment.

I went out with Rama to meet some of her neighbours. Prachi, who had been providing me research assistance, also joined me there. We were invited into a house, not dissimilar to Jahanvi's and Chandni's houses that I had frequented, to meet a young woman called Sarla, whom Rama knew well. We were seated on the bed and were offered drinks. Sarla was soon to be married; she had not been in employment, but she had done a few short-term courses at the nearby Mahila Mandal (Women's Centre, a skill training centre for women) to learn sewing and beauty parlour work. She never tried to monetise skills that she had gained. Sarla told us that she had only studied up to class 4 because of adverse circumstances in her family. And, hence, she did not ever think that employment was an option for her. Her comment reminded me of Jahanvi's mother equating education with employment: '… what if there's a marriage proposal in which the family wants a *padhi-likhi* [educated] girl? Will you ask Jahanvi at *end time* to go earn money then?' It was perhaps the converse of this for Sarla – since she was not educated, she was obviously not going to do a job. Notably, for Rama, the lack of education had not automatically meant lack of employment, but it had restricted her options for employment.

As I was talking to Sarla, several young girls came in and joined us, making up for Sarla's recalcitrance. They were all 10–11 years old and in school; they were very interested in contributing to the 'interview' happening in Sarla's house. Prachi and I asked them about school and what they wanted to do when they were older. Initially, they looked at one another and laughed, maybe a little shy about revealing their aspirations to us. But they quickly got over that hesitation and told us that when they finish school, they would find work. They imagined a future in which they would go to a *job* or regular salaried work: 'Han, job pe jaya karenge' (Yes, we will go to work). Just as they went to school together at that time, they imagined they would have fun going to work together too. One of the girls, thinking further about it, added, 'I'll do a *computer course* to get a good job.' Another one, who had been quiet up to that point, nodded and said, 'Apni life banani hai mujh ko' (I have to make my life).

The young girls' desire to be working professionals in the service economy, preferably in jobs that are IT-based or computer-based, mirrors the popular discourse about youth aspirations in globalising India. The young women who feature in this book, on the other hand, were more critical of the aspirations discourse, likely because they were at the stage where they realised the 'cruel optimism' (Berlant 2011) of such aspirations while negotiating everyday constraints. These constraints were both historical – their families had experienced financial adversity, often from the loss of the male breadwinner's income – and contemporary; although they had acquired education and skills, it did not automatically make them 'proper' or secure middle class. They found themselves relegated to and stuck in the lower end of the service economy. Nevertheless, they asserted new subjectivities on the basis of their participation in the globalising economy through service work, rejecting working-class necessity-driven work, particularly paid domestic work. Then we have women like Rama and Sarla, who have not had access to even the Hindi-medium schooling and distance learning higher education that the interlocutors of this research had, and yet they made different choices about employment. Sarla believed her lack of education charted a path of (unremunerated) domesticity for her, while Rama was propelled into (paid) domestic work when faced with poverty.

These varied accounts of women's working lives highlight the dialectical relationship between gender, caste, class and work. As the discussion here and throughout the book shows, women's decisions about work are influenced by social understandings of work. Among lower-middle-class women in Delhi, being educated and consequently being employed is important, although not without contestation. This significance of education and employment for women has to be placed in the context of socio-economic change in post-1990 India, whereby the emerging service economy offers a semblance of professionalism, but the jobs are highly competitive, largely insecure and underpaid, making multiple incomes a pre-requisite for the maintenance of households in urban areas. Women have noted and reported these shifts in marriage negotiations: while previously it was only men's eligibility that was determined by their employment, increasingly families have also started seeking professional women. The young women of this research often discussed this in terms of changing attitudes towards women's employment, but they also recognised that just as their regular income was valuable in their natal households, so it would be in the households they marry into. Their decisions about employment (and the kind of employment they entered) were, as such, placed in these interrelationships between work and conditions of everyday lives.

Importantly, the women made these decisions not about employment in isolation but more broadly about their working lives. Rama, as a single mother, was propelled into necessity-driven work, but Sarla, even though her family struggled to make ends meet, avoided it and hoped that marriage would offer her security. The young women of this research situated themselves in between: while they did not buy into the promise of security through marriage, they did not entirely forego investment in status production work (Papanek 1979), in part with the understanding that they did not have the choice to not marry. Their in-between-ness or middle-ness, as the book shows, was also demonstrated through distancing themselves from necessity by qualifying their work as skilled and professional while also recognising that they were dependent on and exploited in this insecure low-end service work for the sustenance of upwardly mobile lives. Women's work – including employment, education and skill training, unpaid domestic work and status production work – as such emerges as a significant site for making, unmaking and remaking of social relations and consequently new subjectivities.

Work, inequalities and subjectivities in new India

This book places women at the centre of socio-economic change in India, not just as subjects of globalisation, development and modernity, but as social agents. In particular, the book explores how women position themselves vis-à-vis new work subjectivities. These 'new' subjectivities are not new in the linear sense of the term; rather, they are new in so much as there is reconfiguration of terms, meanings and connotations attached to worker and work-related identities in post-liberalisation India, generated through the friction between old, continuing and new forms of social inequalities. The term 'working', as Chapter 6 explores, used as an identity, carries conflicting social values. On the one hand, women assert themselves as working professionals to signify their place in new India; on the other hand, women are aware of the traces of the historical association between the label 'working women' and promiscuity, immorality and a lack of respectability. To *become* working is, then, contrary to popular discourse of youth aspirations for work in multinational corporations, not a straightforward trajectory, especially when viewed from the vantage point of lower-middle-class women.

Further, from the vantage point of lower-middle-class women, we are also able to see how work identities are constructed and asserted relationally and in interaction with a multitude of fields. In entering service work, women distance themselves from housewives, rejecting domesticity on the premise that they are educated. Their education also puts them in a position to *choose* the kind of work they want to do, escaping the necessity-driven work that their parents may have done. In gendered terms, they particularly refer to their escape from paid domestic work (resonating with Stephanie Lawler's [1999] research on working-class women claiming fragmented middle-class identities through narratives of 'getting out and getting away'). This relationship between education and employment also manifests in their engagement in skill training, not only to find employment but also to while away time when they are in between jobs. At work – in cafés, shopping malls, call centres and offices – women naturally come into interaction with managers. They recognise that the managers are placed above them, not just in the hierarchy of the workplace but also in the social order beyond work. The managers are largely men who have the securities of the middle class that these women cannot access. Even as women's entry into service work may be new, this relationship – whereby women work under the directives of managers – restabilises gender, class and caste norms (McRobbie 2007). However, this re-stabilisation does not go entirely unchallenged.

As we see in Chapter 6, women have their moments of refusal, whereby they retaliate against orders to carry out certain tasks at work, sometimes even quitting work as a result. Their refusal too – an assertion of respectable professional worker identity – is constructed in relation to other workers. Some of the women of this research, for example, refused to wash dishes or clean tables in a café, arguing that this was not part of their job remit; this work was instead supposed to be done by 'housekeepers' and cleaners, largely men, who were placed lower than the women, again both in the professional hierarchy and the social order, in this case specifically by caste. Historically, the work of cleaning has been assigned to people from low castes. Additionally, this work has been feminised. This is not to say that it is always done by women (although that is largely the case around the world), but those who do cleaning are assigned a low position on the gender–caste hierarchy (Kannabiran and Kannabiran 1991), such that the men from low-caste backgrounds are feminised through the mechanism of work. Lower-middle-class women, in taking up service work, traversing public spaces (as discussed in Chapter 3) and resisting what they see as gendered implication into cleaning work may be challenging gender norms, but this challenge is premised on the reiteration of other social norms – in particular, caste norms in this case. Entering masculine spaces, women may indeed assert their distance from cleaning work by relying on its relegation to low caste–class–gender hierarchy.

As women reflect on their in-between position as service professionals – in simplistic terms, with managers and customers secure in their higher status, and with cleaners or housekeepers, the working poor and housewives relegated to a lower position – they also recognise the social trap of new work in new India. In part, women seem to have greater conviction in the potential for service work to set them on a path of upward mobility when initially entering it, but once in work, the sense that there is little room to progress becomes dominant. As the young women of this research narrated, while they were recruited into roles that, adopting global corporate language, promised professionalism through job titles such as 'brew master', 'sales executive' and 'beauty assistant', the actual work practices and work environment were not commensurate with this professed professionalism. 'On the job, nobody even speaks English,' Prachi complained. This complaint emerged on the back of many discussions about how the expectation to speak English is the norm in the service world and how women make concerted efforts to address their lack of fluency in English owing to the Hindi-medium schooling they received and the expectation that they will speak English in service work (as discussed in Chapter 2). There are, as such, clear discrepancies between the discursive constructions and the lived realities of emerging work, as other scholars have also highlighted. Importantly, women's interactions with new subjectivities are tied closely to the conditions of and relations at work, with reference to circulating popular discourses.

The dynamic of young women in professional work – mostly from low- to middle-caste and -class backgrounds – with men in the roles of managers on the one hand and with cleaners and housekeepers on the other reveals multiple social conflicts and (re)configurations. The women assert their professional identities by making intersectional gender, caste and class claims – in relation to managers, gender and class are at the fore, whereas in relation to cleaners and housekeepers, caste and gender (transgressions) are the more potent social categories. While the myth that the new workplaces of new India offer equal opportunities is promoted through popular discourse, the relational formation of work identities shows that they are structured through historical inequalities of gender, class and caste.

Agency, anxiety and reflexivity

The inequalities of and at work tie in with young women workers' future orientations: Can the attempt to become 'ma'am' by speaking English at work pay off in the long run, or are they destined to remain 'madams' to be mocked throughout their lives? Can they be in public spaces – as modern or new Indian women – without being labelled 'heroines' or 'fast-forward', without being judged as sexually promiscuous, improper and 'out of place'

(Patel 2010)? Can they be the aspirational 'middle-class' youth without being disparaged as 'working'? For these young women, new subjectivities are desirable – through them, women assert their agency. They engage in forms of self-fashioning – through speaking English, make-up, clothes and practices of leisure, friendship and romance – that signal their place in the world. Their agency, as such, manifests in narratives of newness, freedom and independence, as the various chapters of the book outline. This crafting of the self is a pleasurable project, but since their place in the world and the world that they are in are in flux, simultaneously changing and unchanging, it is also an unstable and anxiety-generating project (Dickey 2012). In part, the anxiety is generated by women's own sense of the project of self-making being an ongoing, rather than a finished or complete, project. They are aware that the self that they are crafting does not come naturally to them; it is not part of their 'habitus' (Bourdieu 2010 [1984]). They therefore do not have the authority to validate their new selves. While they do not explicitly seek validation from gatekeepers – employers, customers, general public – who constitute the 'proper middle class' and upper class in urban spaces, their consciousness that their selves are vulnerable to judgement is heightened. In part, the anxiety is fuelled by the friction between the new subjectivities that they aspire to and the historically injurious subjectivities that they are ascribed, which they cannot fully escape.

This is, then, their entanglement in processes of value accrual (Skeggs 2014), but specifically in a context where values are in flux. Work is an important site where these contestations emerge; women's participation in the workforce, specifically in emerging service work, is a sign of the nation's modernity and development. But women workers are the obvious outsiders in workspaces. Women are still required to also be housewives – much as young women may reject this subjectivity, they are unable to refuse the responsibility of housework now and in the future – to sustain the mirage of the success of the capitalist market. They and their families may be deemed conservative, traditional or old-fashioned if they are not in employment, but conversely they and their families may be deemed without honour for relying on women's incomes. They may further be chastised for disrupting gendered norms if their employment encroaches on their domestic responsibilities. These varying mechanisms that limit women's self-fashioning, and consequently their agency, highlight how labour performances are closely tied to the performance of gender and, subsequently, how contestations over labour are contestations over social relations.

A theme that runs through women's narratives about their selves is that of *duality*. I specifically use the term 'duality' here to express its varied iterations in subject formations, as the chapters show. While women are keen to learn English, recognising its importance in securing new service work, they *simultaneously* mock one another's efforts to become English. They are critical of those who are conservative in their attitudes towards women's employment, but they also police themselves to assert that their participation in employment is virtuous, demonstrating a *double consciousness* (Cox 2015) of who they want to be and who they are thought to be. They exercise *plasticity* of form (Islam 2022; Malabou 2010; Sanabria 2016) in moulding their appearances to suit various sites: work, neighbourhoods, leisure spaces, and so on. They position themselves *in between* the proper middle class and the working class, disidentifying (Skeggs 1997) from both positions, rather than identifying with one. As they traverse different sites – work, home, leisure – they adapt their selves, effecting *flexible aspirations* (Vijayakumar 2013) to belong at or in these sites. But their adaptations are not limited to variations in the sites that they inhabit. Instead, their aspirations and emerging selves can be formed *and* undermined at the same site – this book shows how women both assert and limit new subjectivities in a process of *mid-identification* at and through the site of work.

Their mid-identification is, then, iterated in varied ways – as simultaneity, contradiction, conflict, in-between-ness, double consciousness, plasticity, compromise, flexibility, and so on, manifesting in the process of making 'middle lives'. The weight of making middle lives – of being actively engaged in the project of modernity, such as through participation in new service work, while also maintaining structures that uphold historical privileges, such as through assigning primacy to the family – falls disproportionately on women (Ganguly-Scrase 2003; John and Gopal 2021; Sarkar 2001). It is not particularly remarkable that their selves are not unitary or coherent – the narrative construction of a 'self' is a *process* of creation and fabrication (Byrne 2003) – but it is important to note that their mid-identification emerges from their experiences of modernity, development and globalisation. This becomes visible in their reflections on the work they are entering. While they invest in the mechanisms that enable entry into new service work – education, skill training, self-transformation – they are also aware that this is simply a game.

Rather than being 'taken in' by the game (Bourdieu 2010 [1984]), they are critical of the futility of the rules of the game. Prachi and Chandni both highlighted that although they were expected to speak fluent English and inhabit corporate comportment to *enter* service work, once they entered work, these skills and appearances were of little use. Moreover, they realised that the work they entered was unable to deliver on its promise of mobility. They could only ever enter low-level service work and found themselves trapped in it, moving horizontally from one kind of work to another, as Chapter 6 in particular shows. In that, while the women attempted to fashion themselves into modern subjects par excellence, their experiences of modernity were subpar at best and fallacious at worst. They realised that institutional and popular discourse offered them a world that was fictitious and, moreover, that its fiction was maintained through their exploitation.

As lower-middle-class women, they enter service work both to symbolise and to seek upward mobility. But with low pay, insecure contracts and less-than-desirable working conditions, the women of this research questioned the tenets of this mobility. They pointed to their managers who came from 'proper' middle-class backgrounds and had already achieved mobility at work by way of progression to highlight the force of societal reproduction (Bhattacharya 2017), particularly the generational reproduction of inequalities. Importantly, they reflected on the longer-term histories of their families – which often included the breakdown of the 'male breadwinner' norm – to account for the limits on their capacity for mobility. Their work sustained not just their families but also mobility of the secure middle class. It is through their *service work* that the secure middle class in India has been able to produce the global youth who are café-going, English-speaking, multinational professionals. In these unequal and varied experiences of globalisation, these young women's participation in work is characterised by agency in the form of assertion of newness, anxiety or worry about their 'lack' and reflexivity leading to critique of globalisation's promise of mobility.

The future of work and workers

In conversations about the desirability for and critique of new service work, and particularly in musing about resigning, the young women who feature in this book identified work that they would like to do. This often came up in response to my question – 'What job would you like to do instead?' – when they shared their will to quit their current jobs. Some women told me what they had *wanted* to do and what they ended up with; Prachi, for example, previously had ambitions to do work that involved 'reading and writing'. As an avid reader and creative writer, she imagined such a job – perhaps in a media house – would be fulfilling. But her ambition was struck down initially when she could not gain admission to 'regular' higher education and had to rely on distance learning instead. She further realised that this work required a high degree of social and cultural capital – one could secure an internship to get started if they have the right contacts, which she, unfortunately, did not. Chandni had tried 'events' work. What had initially seemed like somewhat glamorous and well-paid work turned out to be a scam. Chandni and her friend Chitra were left chasing employers for meagre payments. Based on these experiences, no longer looking for their first jobs, women had developed a better understanding of the work that they would *like to do*. They used two terms to describe these jobs: 'office job' and 'computer job'. Sheela told me, 'If I change jobs, I want an *office job*, where I can work on a *computer*.' When I asked them to elaborate, they often described the material features of such work: it would be based in an air-conditioned office, all workers would have their own desks, and they would work primarily on computers. Some gave examples of what the actual work would entail: data entry and data management; human resources, or HR work; and office administration. There are two points of discussion that emerge from women's future work orientations, which I will discuss in turn as areas for further research.

First, the young women identified 'office jobs' and 'computer jobs' as 'good' jobs partly due to the material conditions of work they offer, particularly in contrast to the material conditions of the work they were doing at the time. In cafés and shopping malls, where women were involved in retail and hospitality work, not only did they do long shifts at work, often six to seven days a week, but they also did these shifts on their feet. This was exacerbated by the exhaustion they incurred on their work commute, usually changing several modes of transport in favour of minimising expenses. Deepti, who worked in a café, said, 'Our whole day goes by just standing up…. My legs are now always swollen. When I lift my legs, they hurt…. It takes half an hour to go to the [bus] stop.' She added, 'Now I'm used to it. When you become used to it, you can't really tell. Like I can't tell anymore.' In the café that I frequented during the early days of fieldwork, I noted that there was no provision for workers to sit down, get changed or take a break. I would usually sit down with my coffee, laptop and notebook while Sheela and Prachi would stand for hours on end, sometimes behind the till, at other times pacing in the café waiting for customers. Sometimes they would complain about headache, back pain or period cramps. More commonly, unease or pain would be expressed through silence and sullenness. In expressing a desire for office or computer work, where they would work sitting at a desk and presumably be paid better, women expressed an understanding of the limits of the body as a resource at work (Wolkowitz 2006).

Second, the type of work that the women wanted to get into is largely representative of emerging work in India. The material is indeed entirely entangled with the symbolic. While at skill centres, the women acquired the know-how for corporate jobs – how to speak English, use computers, wear 'smart' clothing – these courses did not lead to corporate jobs. Disappointed with her café job, Sarita said, 'The thing is, if somebody is doing a *computer course*, they [skill centres] should tell them about computer-related jobs, not about *retail*.' Interestingly, although some of the women had previously worked in call centres and small offices, they did not qualify this as office or computer work, primarily because they had mostly done 'calling work' (calling up customers to sell a product) with unrealistic sales targets and low pay in these workplaces. Office or computer work, they imagined, would be better work in that it would actually be done on a computer. In that, the women considered computer technology as holding promise of better work, which is a prominent theme in the discourse about the future of work in India, divergent from the fear over job losses in the Global North as technology, especially artificial intelligence (AI), makes inroads in the world of work. In part, technology offers women distance from body labour, or work that relies on or involves intensive use of the body as a resource. This is, again, tied in with formations of social relations, with manual work assigned to those low on the hierarchy of the gender–class–caste nexus. In part, technology, as new service work, offers women an entry into the global and modern world (Gupta 2019).

The afterlives

Research persists beyond the confines of fieldwork. But, more importantly, *lives* persist beyond the confines of research. What started out as my doctoral project in mid-2016 has turned into ongoing, long-term ethnography, in part enabled by the ability to keep in touch via digital tools of communication, complemented by regular visits, including extended stays during the Covid-19 pandemic. During this time, much has changed, even as much has remained unchanged. I have become close to three women in particular – Sheela,

Prachi and Chandni. All three of them, after changing many jobs over the years, including several frustrating spells of unemployment, are now working in what can be loosely categorised as office or computer work.

Sheela has found employment as an HR professional for a company that provides ground handling services for airports. She is responsible for processing salary slips for employees spread over several cities in India. When Sheela got a job offer following an interview at this company, she excitedly sent me a video of the office; it is a large open-plan office, air-conditioned throughout, with office desks and chairs allocated to employees. Prachi has been working since before the pandemic at an e-commerce company that supplies dental products to dentists. This came in handy during the pandemic: unlike some of her peers whose work did not lend itself to remote working, Prachi could continue working (from home) and bringing an income throughout the pandemic (Islam 2021). She was recently shifted from the logistics team to the exports team after threatening to quit, citing the lack of progression.

Chandni has been working at a company that manufactures plumbing supplies. Her role involves maintaining the database of and coordinating service delivery with plumbers. She has been doing the same work for a while and has felt frustrated with the lack of avenues for growth. Perhaps to channel that frustration, Chandni has become active on social media with a view to becoming an influencer who is paid for product promotions. She started with posting TikTok-style videos – lip syncing and dancing to popular songs – and has since graduated to posting make-up tutorials and reviews of beauty products. The work that Sheela, Prachi and Chandni are now doing reflects shifts in the composition of 'new service work', a term that I have used loosely throughout the book. While work in malls, cafés and call centres was still relatively new in 2016 when I began this fieldwork, I am not sure if it can still be qualified as 'new' anymore. Rather, it is work at e-commerce companies and start-ups and work through social media that has, within a decade, overtaken retail and hospitality work as 'new' and desirable work. In keeping with this, there is now emerging research on digital work, and my own work has, in part, moved in this direction.

It is also notable that despite edging into their late 20s now, Sheela, Prachi and Chandni are still managing to resist pressure from their families to get married. Sheela explicitly noted that there is less urgency around her marriage because of the significance of her income to the upkeep of her family. Prachi's elder sister is not yet married, so she has some breathing space, but notably she is also the main and only stable earner for her family. Chandni is in a relationship, which her parents know about, but she does not feel ready for marriage. Although her brother is now also in work, it is primarily her income that contributes towards household expenses. While retaining the job that she does not like, but that nevertheless pays, she is focusing on developing her career as an influencer or social media entrepreneur.

They – the young women of and in new India – are in the process of making their lives.

References

Berlant, Lauren. 2011. *Cruel Optimism*. Durham (NC) and London: Duke University Press.

Bhattacharya, Tithi (ed.). 2017. *Social Reproduction Theory: Remapping Class, Recentering Oppression*. London: Pluto Press.

Bourdieu, Pierre. 2010 (1984). *Distinction: A Social Critique of the Judgement of Taste*. Abingdon and Oxon: Routledge.

Byrne, Bridget. 2003. 'Reciting the Self: Narrative Representations of the Self in Qualitative Interviews'. *Feminist Theory* 4(1): 29–49. DOI: 10.1177/1464700 103004001002.

Cox, Aimee Meredith. 2015. *Shapeshifters: Black Girls and the Choreography of Citizenship*. Durham, NC: Duke University Press.

Dickey, Sara. 2012. 'The Pleasures and Anxieties of Being in the Middle: Emerging Middle-Class Identities in Urban South India'. *Modern Asian Studies* 46(3): 559–99.

Ganguly-Scrase, Ruchira. 2003. 'Paradoxes of Globalization, Liberalization, and Gender Equality: The Worldviews of the Lower Middle Class in West Bengal, India'. *Gender and Society* 17(4): 544–66.

Gupta, Hemangini. 2019. 'Testing the Future: Gender and Technocapitalism in Start-Up India'. *Feminist Review* 123(1): 74–88. DOI: 10.1177/01417789 19879740.

Islam, Asiya. 2021. '"Two Hours Extra for Working from Home": Reporting on Gender, Space, and Time from the Covid-Field of Delhi, India'. *Gender, Work and Organization* 28 (S2 Supplement: Feminist Frontiers): 405–14. DOI: 10.1111/gwao.12617.

———. 2022. 'Plastic Bodies: Women Workers and Emerging Body Rules in Service Work in Urban India'. *Gender and Society* 36(3): 422–44. DOI: 10.1177/08912432221089637.

John, Mary E., and Meena Gopal (eds.). 2021. *Women in the Worlds of Labour: Interdisciplinary and Intersectional Perspectives*. New Delhi: Orient Blackswan.

Kannabiran, Vasanth, and Kalpana Kannabiran. 1991. 'Caste and Gender: Understanding Dynamics of Power and Violence'. *Economic and Political Weekly* 26(37): 2130–33.

Lawler, Stephanie. 1999. '"Getting Out and Getting Away": Women's Narratives of Class Mobility'. *Feminist Economics* 63(1): 3–24.

Malabou, Catherine. 2010. *Plasticity at the Dusk of Writing*. New York, NY: Columbia University Press.

McRobbie, Angela. 2007. 'TOP GIRLS? Young Women and the Post-Feminist Sexual Contract1'. *Cultural Studies* 21(4–5): 718–37. DOI: 10.1080/095023 80701279044.

Papanek, Hanna. 1979. 'Family Status Production: The "Work" and "Non-Work" of Women'. *Signs: Journal of Women in Culture and Society* 4(4): 775–81.

Patel, Reena. 2010. *Working the Night Shift: Women in India's Call Center Industry*. Redwood City, CA: Stanford University Press.

Sanabria, Emilia. 2016. *Plastic Bodies: Sex Hormones and Menstrual Suppression in Brazil*. Durham, NC: Duke University Press.

Sarkar, Tanika. 2001. *Hindu Wife, Hindu Nation: Community, Religion, and Cultural Nationalism*. Bloomington, IN: Indiana University Press.

Skeggs, Bev. 2014. 'Values beyond Value? Is Anything beyond the Logic of Capital?' *British Journal of Sociology* 65(1): 1–20. DOI: 10.1111/1468-4446.12072.

Skeggs, Beverley. 1997. *Formations of Class and Gender: Becoming Respectable*. London: Sage Publications.

Vijayakumar, Gowri. 2013. '"I'll Be Like Water"'. *Gender and Society* 27(6): 777–98. DOI: 10.1177/0891243213499445.

Wolkowitz, Carol. 2006. *Bodies at Work*. London: Sage Publications.

Index